Ghostly Lighthouses
from
Maine to Florida

GHOSTLY LIGHTHOUSES

FROM

MAINE TO FLORIDA

Sheryl Monks

John F. Blair, Publisher  *Winston-Salem, North Carolina*

*The paper in this book meets the guidelines
for permanence and durability of the Committee on
Production Guidelines for Book Longevity
of the Council on Library Resources.*

Cover Image
Cape Hatteras Lighthouse with full moon by Joe McLear
© Joe McLear / TRANSPARENCIES, Inc.

Library of Congress Cataloging-in-Publication Data

Monks, Sheryl, 1967–
Ghostly lighthouses from Maine to Florida / by Sheryl Monks.
p.   cm.
ISBN-13: 978-0-89587-310-1
ISBN-10: 0-89587-310-9 (alk. paper)
1. Ghosts—United States. 2. Haunted places—United States. 3.
Lighthouses—United States—Miscellanea. I. Title.

BF1472.U6M64 2005
133.1'22—dc22
2005005219

Design by Debra Long Hampton
Composition by The Roberts Group

For
Bruce.

And for Mom and Dad.

CONTENTS

Preface   ix

Unchanged Melody   3
Seguin Island Light, near Popham Beach, Maine

The Lobsterman of Wood Island   15
Wood Island Light, Biddeford Pool, Maine

The Abiding Bride   23
Boon Island Light, near York, Maine

The Portuguese Phantom   39
Minot's Ledge Light, near Scituate, Massachusetts

The Curse of the Pirate Light Keeper   47
Bird Island Light, Marion, Massachusetts

Yearning Ernie   57
New London Ledge Light, New London, Connecticut

America's Most Haunted Lighthouse   65
Point Lookout Light, Chesapeake Bay, Maryland

The North Room   73
Currituck Beach Light, Corolla, North Carolina

The Disappearance of Theodosia 79
Cape Hatteras Light, Buxton, North Carolina

The Young Guardian 91
Georgetown Light (North Island Light),
near Georgetown, South Carolina

The Bloodstained Floor 97
Cape Romain Light,
near McClellanville, South Carolina

The Blue Lady of Leamington 105
Old Hilton Head Rear Range Light
(Leamington Light),
Hilton Head, South Carolina

A Grievous Passion 117
St. Simons Island Light, near Brunswick, Georgia

The Little Sisters of St. Augustine 129
St. Augustine Light, Anastasia Island, Florida

The Poltergeist of Pensacola 135
Pensacola Light, Pensacola Bay, Florida

Acknowledgments 143

PREFACE

The challenge in writing a collection of stories about ghostly lighthouses, I found, is twofold. First, the job requires a good deal of research, but in the end, nothing can really be proven. Second, the stories are presumably at least partly fictitious, though there are boundaries to how far they can be spun.

Before I explain, let me tell you why I was compelled to write this book in the first place. Unlike the many writers who claim to have sprung from a family of voracious readers, I freely admit that I don't recall being read bedtime stories very much as a child. Until I entered school, books were not commonplace in our home, though I believe ours was one filled with all the right elements for developing an early love of literature.

My mother sang stories to my younger siblings and me, old Appalachian ballads that spoke of murder and mayhem— "Pretty Polly," "Patches," "Tom Dooley." My paternal grandmother—who claimed to be part Cherokee and swore her youngest daughter was once small enough to fit inside a mayonnaise jar—told, as you might guess, tall tales. Indeed, she told the tallest of tall tales. She called them yarns. My mother called them big, fat whoppers.

My father, too, can tell a whopper now and then. But the stories I most often heard him tell were far better than even my grandmother's wacky fables. Her stories would send me to unimagined places and thrill me with implausible adventures. Dad's stories sent me somewhere else—to his childhood home in Elkton, Maryland. His stories spoke of a *real* place and a *real* time not too distant. Only the goings-on he swore he'd witnessed there were unfathomable—headless ghosts unbolting doors, headlights of driverless cars shining into the house as they came up the driveway, rugs that cried if they were kicked under the bed, shoes that walked themselves back to the trash dump where they'd been found, lights flickering mysteriously, eerie apparitions sinking into the solid slabs of rock they stood upon.

I took on this project because I am a fan of ghost stories. To my mind, the ghost story far surpasses the tall tale and other folk stories. For all its exaggeration and humor and imaginative leaps and good, old-fashioned fun, the tall tale simply can't compare to a well-told ghost story. Unlike the tall tale, which we know from the outset is preposterous, the ghost tale is sworn to be true. There's something eminently more fascinating about the possible truth of things unimagined or unbelievable. We want badly to believe in the inexplicable. When I was a kid, ghost stories were spoken as the gospel truth. I never doubted a word my father told me—and it wasn't because I was a child and didn't know any better. His eyewitness accounts were proof enough that ghosts really existed. Though I had not yet seen one myself, it seemed I soon would.

Even today, ghost stories endure. Modern ghost trackers use expensive, high-tech gadgets that claim to be sensitive enough to monitor and record paranormal activity. Even so, skeptics are suspicious of pictures of floating orbs and other evidence that appears as if it could have been manufactured. Ghosts are about the only unsolved mysteries we have left. Despite all our technological savvy, we are as clueless about them today as we've ever been.

But it's a conundrum we never want resolved. Though

we yearn for irrefutable evidence to put an end to the question, therein lies the spell a ghost story casts over us as well. Conflicting "facts" only add to the ghost story's appeal.

Lighthouses offer the perfect settings for ghost stories because their whole reason for being derived from the grim and very real prospect of death. They are beautiful, their purpose noble. But there's something confounding about them as well.

Like castles, to which they are often compared, historic lighthouses are cold, damp fortresses. They were built to withstand destructive forces—usually the awesome might of the sea but occasionally the armies of men, as happened on several occasions during the Civil War. They were constructed in the most dangerous locations—sometimes right in the very places of which they warned. Access, quite obviously, was limited, the only contact from the outside world coming in the form of tenders that ferried supplies to lighthouse families. The Lighthouse Service—also referred to in this book as the Lighthouse Establishment and the Lighthouse Board, depending on the period of the organization's history—provided everything a family needed. Only on occasion was it necessary to leave the isolation of the light station—say, to fetch a doctor from the mainland. Otherwise, light keepers lived with only the companionship of their families—if they were so lucky to be stationed where that was possible. Some were virtually imprisoned at their remote outposts. More than a few went mad.

But perhaps what fascinates us most about lighthouses is that they are by and large becoming obsolete. Though many still stand as reminders of a gallant past, others are falling into disrepair or being replaced by more modern navigational aids. Luckily, lighthouse enthusiasts abound. Many volunteer organizations have stepped forward to restore and preserve beacons all around the country.

On the most basic level, ghost stories speak to our

childhood fears of death. Dr. John Davis, professor of folk studies at the Institute of Texan Culture, believes that they are much more than that, however, arguing that ghost tales are a part of a community's history as vital as oral interviews and photographs. "Like all stories," he says, "they are mirrors." Clearly, then, lighthouse ghost stories are meant to summon the fears most common to coastal communities—the dread of isolation, of terrifying weather conditions, of death by drowning.

In writing these fifteen tales, I felt a responsibility to preserve them as they have been handed down through generations. But in keeping with the oral tradition from which ghost tales arose, I also felt obligated to tell each story in the most compelling fashion possible. In so doing, I hope I have presented them in the spirit in which they were intended to be told. I don't know if the stories herein are true. I've done my best to verify what can be verified and taken the rest on faith. Perhaps we'll never know with any certainty.

As for me, I hope we never do.

GHOSTLY LIGHTHOUSES
FROM
MAINE TO FLORIDA

Seguin Island Light
© *2004 Bob and Sandra Shanklin, the "Lighthouse People"*

UNCHANGED MELODY

SEGUIN ISLAND LIGHT
NEAR POPHAM BEACH, MAINE

"Alas! all music jars when the soul's out of tune."

Miguel de Cervantes, *Don Quixote*

Seguin Island is one of the foggiest locations in the country. One year, it was plagued by fog 31 percent of the time. Imagine living for so long in such a haze, fixing your eyes on a world rarely extending beyond what is immediately before you. One is bound to feel isolated—even light keepers accustomed to being cut off from the world.

Now, add to that image the forlorn sound of a foghorn warning others to stay away. As is common all along the coast of Maine, a dangerous ledge sits near Seguin Island, threatening passing ships. Even in calm weather, the rumble of the surf once demanded horns that sounded ceaselessly.

That weather conditions affect our moods is no great discovery. Consider how long we've used the expression "feeling under the weather," or think of how we describe someone as having a "sunny disposition." New research in the field of biometeorology—the study of the effects of weather on life—has identified a condition called Seasonal Affective Disorder, which causes bouts of depression in people during the light-deprived months or in other instances when they are exposed to extended periods of darkness. Though we don't often perceive it, cloud coverage, rain, and fog are all factors that can alter our moods. Amazingly, meteorology is so advanced in some parts of Europe that forecasters can actually identify specific areas where weather conditions are likely to make people become neurotic—or even psychotic!

Perhaps this was what plagued the wife of a nineteenth-century lighthouse keeper at Seguin Island. The story goes that until she arrived on the island with her husband, she was a bonny bride quick to smile and quicker still to play a tune on her pianoforte. Hers was a fine-made Broadwood upright, and though she hadn't the talent for playing tunes by ear, she was a faithful student. It overjoyed her simply to play and to hear the melody the instrument made.

But moving to the island meant she had to leave her prized piano, for it was too large to transport on the small tender that ferried the couple to its new home. And even if there had been room aboard, the instrument would have proven difficult to carry up the steep hill to the keeper's residence. Though she was quite fond of it, she left the upright behind without quarrel, for she was more enthusiastic about her husband's new post as light keeper than anything else.

To prove her allegiance to a life at sea, the keeper's wife assisted her husband whenever she could, hauling up coal from the hopper at the bottom of the tramway to save him the effort. She also helped him polish the brass and draw the curtain around the majestic first-order Fresnel lens to protect it from sunlight. In the evenings, she prepared their meals. But after a while, she found the same old foods provided by the Lighthouse Service rather dull. "Wouldn't it be nice," she said one day to her husband, "to grow our own vegetables, to raise our own hens and goats?"

"That'd be fine," her husband said. And the next week, he sent for seed and whatever livestock she desired.

"Just a few laying hens," she said. "And three or four handsome dairy goats would be nice for making milk soap and body butters. I fear this wind will chafe me bad come winter." Already, her slender fingers had become calloused by the work she performed out-of-doors, though the good wife did not complain.

And so it happened that for a few solid weeks, the weather held and she planted a large garden of asparagus, blueberries, raspberries, garlic, pumpkins, corn, melons, herbs, and greens. Each day before dusk, she called her husband to come for a look at her progress, taking delight in every creeping tendril that broke from the ground.

"You've a green thumb, m'dear," her husband said, smiling. His simple admiration of the garden pleased her. Soon, she was able to treat him to breakfasts of fresh eggs and goat's milk.

But nothing lasts forever.

Before long, a glowering fog set in that made itself at home on the island both day and night. Even without rain or drizzling winds carried up from the sea, the ground was oversupplied with condensation that clung to trees and edifices and slowly dribbled down, leaching toward the earth. Without proper sunlight, plants slowly began to rot in the rows where they'd sprouted. True daylight seemed but a muddled reminiscence, for the sky was fixed in perpetual dusk.

Accustomed to rising early, the keeper's wife soon began waiting till noon to try and make her way from the house to the garden plot. She often found herself lost, either teetering dangerously close to the cliffs above Seguin Cove or heading in the direction of Hunnewell Beach.

Neglected, the garden was choked by weeds until she stopped hoping for its recovery and forgot it altogether. Then she was left with nothing but the chickens and the goats. And because she had not penned them in, they became impossible to locate in the cheating light. Sometimes, she found an egg in the same spot twice, but never three times, though she searched diligently every morning. She could no longer manage even such a little thing as breakfast. Off in the distance, she heard the hens clucking and the goats bleating, but she caught sight of none, not even when she scraped together a handful of cracked corn to throw to the animals. Just as the garden had gone to seed, the animals became wild as the seabirds that hovered just out of sight in the clotted sky.

No longer did she pull the curtain around the great Fresnel lens in the lighthouse, for the hazard the sun had once presented was no longer a concern. And while her husband was kept busier than ever, she had no desire to assist him with his duties. She found herself becoming increasingly irritable should he ask her to haul up coal in the hopper or light a fire in the fog signal house. "That blasted foghorn is driving me mad," she protested, complaining that it was the cause of the rash of maladies she'd recently suffered—everything from migraines and anxiety to nausea and sleeplessness.

Despite the challenge of crossing the river in such fog, her husband insisted they take a short trip to the mainland, where he bought her a handsome set of tin stencils made in nearby Biddeford. The stencils allowed patterns to be transferred onto burlap, helping one create hooked rugs with highly decorative designs. She had once been fond of making bed rugs, so the whimsical cutouts of animals and geometric shapes brought a smile to her face again. The keeper was pleased.

But it was not to last.

Staying indoors had a negative effect on the keeper's wife. Complaining of too little light to work on the rugs, she tossed the embroidery aside and took to staying in bed for days on end, until the light keeper grew quite concerned for her health. "Not feeling well, m'dear?" he would ask. But she never replied.

One day when the tender crept through the mist with supplies and the local weekly, the keeper saw a circular advertising spinet piano kits for sale with one accompanying sheet of music. Song choices included "I Have a Silent Sorrow Here," "King of the Sea," "Oh, Whisper What Thou Feelest," "Come, Dearest, the Daylight Is Gone," and others, from which the keeper narrowed his selection to two: "Yes, Methinks I See Her Smiling" and "The Banks of the Blue Moselle." He agreed to take whichever was in stock.

When the tender arrived the following week, it brought a brand-new spinet. It was boxed neatly in a small crate that just fit the cart on the tramway, so he was able to haul it up the hillside with little effort.

The light keeper was beside himself with excitement. How clever he was! A new piano would be all it took to wake his wife from her melancholic stupor. The house simply needed music. It was what she had been accustomed to. Why hadn't he thought of it earlier?

He quickly assembled the spinet, a smaller instrument than she had played previously, though it was quite sturdy and certainly enough to fill the house with the sounds of music and his wife's long-lost laughter.

And indeed, it did the trick.

"The Banks of the Blue Moselle"—she held the sheet of music to her bosom and shined a smile so sweet it brought tears to the light keeper's eyes and a silent prayer of gratitude to his worried heart. "Play for me," he said. "Play! Play!" And he danced as best he could to the gay tune of "The Banks of the Blue Moselle."

After she finished, he didn't have to ask for a repeat performance. She fervently played again and again throughout the night, until the tune accompanied their dreams when at last she and her husband went to sleep.

When she awoke next morning, she was more rested than she had been in months. And as luck would have it, the sun was back, shining its light on all the lovely life of Seguin Island. She found the goats and chickens roaming loose and set to devising a plan for penning them so they wouldn't be lost from her again. She tied the goats to the porch railing and closed the chickens up inside the kitchen until she could have the tender bring her stakes and fence wire. Then, after breakfast, she was back at the spinet practicing "The Banks of the Blue Moselle."

Outside, her husband heard the tinkling of piano music and set about happily performing his chores of repainting the lantern room and carrying up fuel for the night ahead.

Plink-plinkle-plink. She played all the day long. Then, as soon as she'd cooked the evening meal and scrubbed the plates, she played again.

After a few days of hearing his wife perform the same sheet of music over and over and over, however, the light keeper wondered how long it would take her to abandon "The Banks of the Blue Moselle" for some other tune, perhaps one she remembered from the songbook she'd left behind with the pianoforte. To encourage her, he said, "I think you've mastered 'The Banks of the Blue Moselle,' m'dear. Know you any other tune?"

She stopped playing and wrinkled her brow in contemplation. "Why, I believe . . ." And she broke off to try some other melody she remembered vaguely. *Plunk-tinkle-plink* went the keys. "No, no," she said. "That isn't it. Not at all." She tried again, but the spinet reverberated with sounds unlike any song the keeper had ever heard.

"That's fine," he said, however, for he enthusiastically

preferred even that wretched effort to another performance of "The Banks of the Blue Moselle." He really didn't care for the tune as much as he thought and wouldn't mind if he never heard it again. "I'll have a smoke and leave you to it," he said, stepping outside. Lighting his pipe, he climbed the tower, for he liked nothing better than the tranquility of seeing the water from such a vantage point and enjoying his tobacco. His thoughts returned to the time when his wife's playing had seemed a wonderment to him. Such a gifted lass. How could she not remember a single tune from the hundreds she once played?

That night, he was mercifully spared another rendition of "The Banks of the Blue Moselle." His wife tried earnestly to recall the notes of an old favorite, "Thou Art So Near and Yet So Far." She hummed the tune to try to find the proper key, but she had never been any good at storing music in her head. She'd loved her old songbook and expected never to be parted from it. Why bother setting the tunes to memory?

But now she was aggrieved. *I must be a simpleton*, she thought. *Even animals perform routine skills from memory. Look how dogs drive sheep.* She remembered hearing of a traveling carnival act in which a chimpanzee performed magic tricks. How could a chimpanzee remember dozens of antics but she could not recall even one of the tunes she had played scores of times in her life?

She tried to remember if she'd ever really set her mind to the task. *No*, she thought. *Not really.* She looked at the sheet of music before her—"The Banks of the Blue Moselle." She would learn to play the tune by heart if it killed her.

The next morning, the tender carefully maneuvered its way around the Pond Island bar, on which many a vessel had come to grief. The small boat carried the fence wire the keeper's wife had requested for the hens. But when her husband carried it up to the house and told her of it, he was waved away so she could resume playing the tune. The keeper cringed at the sound, then mocked it. "The Banks of the Bloody Blue Moselle," he chided.

Oh, how he despised that infernal tune! It was driving his poor wife mad. She hadn't even bothered to fix his breakfast that morn. He'd had only coffee, and that he'd prepared himself. And he was sure that when he returned for the noon meal, he would find her still there at the spinet. He'd be left to forage like the animals running loose.

When he opened the door to leave, he shooed out the hens. "Go on, now," he spat, "before I have you for supper." But one ran confused back toward him. On impulse, he grabbed it up and wrung its neck. Then he threw the bird on the table. "Gave you fair warning," he said. "To blazes with eggs once a fortnight."

Ordinarily, his wife would have been cross with him for killing the hen. But the woman sharing quarters with him of late was no more than a stranger. Stealing a glance inside the parlor, he saw her playing the spinet feverishly. Was she overjoyed? Or was he surveying a madwoman? He fled, snatching up the hen as he went in search of his ax.

But even as he walked beyond the stubby tower in the direction of the shed, the melody slid along behind him. He threw the hen on the trunk of a felled tree and entered the building. But he could not busy his mind against the unrelenting music that infiltrated his brain. Should he throw himself into the sea, even still he would find no relief from the abominable noise. Slamming the door of the shed behind him, he looked furiously for the ax. His wife was not herself, poor woman.

And neither was he.

The keeper's wife turned over the sheet of music and beamed. She had finally mastered the piece and couldn't wait to show her husband. Perhaps she could now successfully summon up other tunes she'd once known. Or maybe she would ask the tender to bring her a new songbook, from which she would commit to memory every tune, so she would never again have to rely on reading music from parchment.

When her husband returned, she called for him to sit and listen. "I've memorized it," she explained, fixing her fingers on the keys and executing the song perfectly, gleefully, proudly. "The Banks of the Blue Moselle" rang out ardently, reverberating through the house until it was drawn out the opened windows by a frenzied storm gathering down at the cove. Waves beat fiercely against the rocks, and the sky darkened over the keeper's residence.

How cheerful the music was, how raucous! "Isn't it magnificent?" she said, not minding the wind slicing through the room, giving wing to the single sheet of music. She found it amusing, in fact, and burbled into laughter, singing the words of the tune as she played louder and faster while her husband approached from behind. " 'In the star-ry light of a sum-mer's night . . .' "

"She isn't herself," the keeper mumbled as he skulked closer.

Her breath came in brisk pants that seemed paced by the jaunty refrain: " 'On the banks of the blue Moselle. On the banks of the blue Moselle.' "

Before him, his wife lifted and lowered her shoulders in bouncy rhythm as she played. He wished she'd sit still. "Stop doing that," he said in a defeated whisper. He watched her shoulders ripple and roll in snappy fashion. How easily he could smash the bones with his bare hands, the teasing bones of her shoulders that so enjoyed the music. So enjoyed it!

" 'On the banks of the Blue Moselle. On the banks of the Blue Moselle.' "

He raised the ax and hastened to silence the blaring spinet. After sinking the weapon into the instrument's flesh, he turned to his wife, and the astonishment of it so staggered her that she shrieked. The pitch sounded to the keeper strangely similar to "The Banks of the Blue Moselle." He studied her neck, the muscles that stretched like piano wire to make the notes that pierced his wits. A black hood of madness wrinkled his face as he raised the blade once more and silenced the house forever.

Or maybe not.

Old folks say that ever since the keeper chopped up his wife and then did away with himself, strange sounds have been heard drifting across the bay at Seguin Island. Some say it's just the squall of a woeful wind. But others swear it's the eerie tinkling of piano music.

Seguin Island Lighthouse, commissioned by George Washington himself in 1795, is listed on the National Register of Historic Places. One of the oldest lighthouses in the country, it is the last light north of Virginia with a first-order Fresnel lens operating continuously since its inception. Sitting at the mouth of the Kennebec River, the island encompasses sixty-four acres of steep, hilly land. Because the island rises 140 feet above sea level, the lighthouse tower is short. Still, it is the highest above sea level in Maine, standing at a combined height of 186 feet above the sea. Today, the grounds include the lighthouse tower connected to a double keepers' residence, a fog signal building, an oil house, a boathouse, and an operating 1,100-foot tramway.

In 1985, the light was automated. A year later, the Friends of Seguin Island organization was incorporated to maintain the historic property. One side of the keepers' house is now a museum displaying artifacts and photos of the light station. The other serves as the residence of the volunteer caretakers who look after the lighthouse from Memorial Day through Labor Day. The present tower stands fifty-three feet tall. It was built in 1857 to replace an earlier one. The Fresnel lens casts light twenty miles out to sea from a single 750-watt bulb.

In 1998, the Fresnel lens came close to being replaced by a modern solar-powered optic when the Coast Guard announced that it was no longer cost-effective to maintain the seventeen-thousand-foot underwater cable necessary to power the light. The Friends of Seguin Island mounted a drive to keep the historic apparatus, collecting more than seventy-two hundred signatures. That effort saved the last continuously operational first-order Fresnel lens in New England.

To reach Seguin Island by boat, it is useful to consult area cruising guides. The Friends of Seguin Island recommend NOAA chart 13295, *Kennebec and Sheepscot River Entrances*. When you enter the cove, you do so at your own risk. There are no dock facilities, so you'll need to bring a dinghy or swim ashore. Be careful, as the rocks are extremely slippery.

You can schedule a summer trip to the island by calling the Maine Maritime Museum in Bath at 207-443-1316. Tours are also available from nearby Popham Beach and Freeport. Organized tours are offered by a number of local charter services. For more information, contact the Friends of Seguin Island by calling 207-443-4808 or by e-mailing keeper@seguinisland.org.

Wood Island Light
© *2004 Bob and Sandra Shanklin, the "Lighthouse People"*

THE LOBSTERMAN OF WOOD ISLAND

WOOD ISLAND LIGHT
BIDDEFORD POOL, MAINE

"O, my offence is rank, it smells to heaven."

William Shakespeare, *Hamlet*

Chances are, when you think of the state of Maine, you think of lobster. Maybe it's because New England is known for the ice-cold waters that allow the creatures to thrive. As early as 1605, fishermen discovered the great bounty Maine had to offer, although commercial selling of lobsters did not begin until around 1840. At that time, there was no means for shipping live shellfish, so the industry relied heavily on canning facilities. By 1895, however, methods of distribution improved significantly. Canning operations soon became a thing of the past, and fresh Maine lobster became the nation's new *pièce de résistance*.

It was about that time when a lobsterman named Fred Milliken and his wife moved from Biddeford Pool to Wood Island, a thirty-six-acre island at the mouth of the Saco River perhaps best known as the home of the Wood Island Lighthouse. Expecting the fishing to be good close to the lobster grounds, Milliken built a house on the west side of the island on property belonging to his uncle. The lobsterman was in his early thirties. Possessing remarkable physical stature and strength, he was considered by some a giant. According to old-timers, he was strong enough to carry his fifteen-foot dory across his shoulders.

If Milliken was a giant, he was a gentle one, for his work required patience as well as stamina. Withstanding severe weather, he trawled close to the shores where lobsters migrated during the summer. Each day, he rowed out to the buoys identifying his traps and hauled them up one by one. Tossing back the "shorts" and any "berried" females—that is, those carrying eggs—he then rebaited the pots with salted herring or some other delicacy and replaced them on the ocean floor. Day in and day out, he spent his life in quiet contemplation—of the rugged beauty of his beloved Maine, of the perseverance of the prehistoric creatures he pulled to the surface of the sea, of the age of the ocean and all its mystique.

Staring back at the island, Milliken sometimes wondered how the place had taken the name Wood Island, seeing as how there was hardly a tree to be found anywhere on it. A series of storms and a devastating fire had left the landscape barren.

The open expanse afforded the lobsterman a clear view of his humble dwelling and the surrounding area, where he often spotted his wife hanging laundry on a line or scrubbing his clothes against the rocks that dotted the seashore.

For a time, folks say, it was a good, simple life—a wholesome young couple living off the land against the romantic backdrop of the ocean and the majestic beacon flashing in the distance.

Nearby lived the lighthouse keeper and his family. Thomas Henry Orcutt and his son George lived with their dog Sailor, a border collie said to possess near-human intelligence. The dog was something of a local celebrity with the fishermen of Biddeford Pool. Passing the island, mariners commonly sounded a bell to salute the light keeper—a gesture quickly answered in kind by Sailor, who rose to his feet, ran to the station's fog bell, and clanged a reply by pulling the rope with his teeth or nudging the bell with his paws.

When he could, the lobsterman spent time with Sailor and his master, dropping by the keeper's house to thaw his hands and feet before heading home to his wife. Keeper Orcutt hung Milliken's wet coat by the fire to dry and filled him with steaming mugs of saffron tea or spiced berry cider. Always neighborly, Milliken insisted on repaying the favor by helping the light keeper with an occasional chore or two. He unburdened Orcutt of the heavy oil cans he had to carry up to the lantern room. "Here, now, old-timer," the lobsterman teased, hoisting the barrels easily.

Milliken had a strong sense of civic duty as well. He was a special police officer and game warden. According to an article by Harold Hanson in a local newspaper called *Quahog*, a great number of seals inhabited the islands off the coast of Maine and New Hampshire at that time. The animals presented such a problem that bounties were paid to hunters to thin the population. Maine paid a dollar to anyone who proved a seal had been slain by producing the animal's nose. New Hampshire required the tails, an inconsistency that allowed bounty hunters to collect money from both states for a single kill. It was this manner of doing business outside the rules that separated most bounty hunters from those who fished and hunted with a sense of respect for their game and for the rule of law.

When the bounty season rolled round in 1896, a man named Howard Hobbs and another named William Moses came to live at Wood Island in a run-down chicken coop alongside the house belonging to Milliken and his wife. Hobbs had no apparent means of earning a living, although he was said to fish on occasion or trap lobsters whenever he needed cash. According to Harold Hanson, however, Hobbs and Moses were bounty hunters whom Milliken was duty-bound to keep an eye on. One thing is certain: Hobbs was known mostly for his drunkenness. Accounts written by Alfred Elden, a local reporter in the 1920s and 1930s, describe Hobbs as a "dissolute chap without visible means of support" who "squatted" in a shack that had once been a henhouse, who worked only to "keep from starving and to maintain his liquor supply."

Legend has it that after living on the island for a time, Hobbs rowed over to the mainland one summer afternoon and tied one on at Old Orchard Beach. Harold Hanson claims that Moses accompanied Hobbs, and that the two spent several hours drinking and raising a ruckus before they were run off by the law. The next day, they crossed the river to Hill's Beach and again set about getting tanked. After spending all their money on the two-day binge, the pair threw themselves into a dinghy and set sail for their hovel back at Wood Island.

It's easy to imagine how the bounty hunter's habits disrupted the quiet lifestyle of the families living peacefully on the island. The lobsterman and the light keeper discussed how best to handle the problem. They agreed that the lobsterman's size might persuade the two bounty hunters to keep their cavorting away from the island. And it was also part of his job as a police officer to ensure the peace. It was thus decided that Milliken should stand waiting for them at the dock when they came staggering out of their boat, telling crude jokes in loud voices and singing vulgar songs.

"How ya do, boys?" the lobsterman said.

"How we do, Moses?" Hobbs asked his companion.

"Oh, we do very well," said Moses, laughing and stumbling up the bank.

Milliken noticed then that Hobbs was carrying a shotgun. "You're in no shape to be handling that," he said, offering to carry the weapon. Hobbs refused.

Because of his size and strength, Milliken was not the sort of man who feared much of anything. He left the men and returned home to fetch his police badge. A short time later, he came back ready to take the gun from Hobbs or else place the men under arrest. He met them on the road home. "Is that gun loaded?" he asked.

"No," Hobbs said. "It isn't."

"I'll see whether it is or not," said Milliken, stepping toward the drunken Hobbs.

As the burly lobsterman approached, Hobbs raised the shotgun and fired, striking the giant in the midsection. Milliken fell. Hearing the shot, Mrs. Milliken came running to her husband's aid. She and William Moses carried the bleeding lobsterman home. Mrs. Milliken then sent Moses to fetch the doctor back in Biddeford Pool.

Meanwhile, Hobbs sobered up and realized what he'd done. Filled with regret, he offered to do whatever he could to help. When the lobsterman complained about his feet hurting, Hobbs reached to pull off the dying man's boots. But Mrs. Milliken refused. "Don't you touch him," she said. "Just leave us be!"

Hobbs raised the shotgun again, this time at the lobsterman's wife. "I just want to loosen his boots." Mrs. Milliken didn't say another word as her husband's attacker unfastened the laces of his boots and gently pulled them off.

Later, Hobbs paced back and forth outside the Milliken house, waiting for Moses to return with the doctor. But forty-five minutes after the shooting, Milliken died.

Overcome with guilt, the bounty hunter decided to turn himself in to the lighthouse keeper. Still carrying his shotgun, he made his way to the keeper's house, where he explained to Thomas Orcutt what had transpired. The keeper implored Hobbs to turn himself in to the authorities on the mainland. Then Orcutt and his son raced to the Milliken house, though it was already too late.

Left alone in the light keeper's house, Hobbs started back home soon thereafter, apparently in a lather. He returned to his little shack out near Milliken's place. Moments later, he played both judge and executioner to himself, laying the shotgun to his head and pulling the trigger.

Many believe this murder-suicide accounts for the strange goings-on at Wood Island. The Milliken house and the old henhouse are grown over in a sea of poison ivy. The lighthouse and the keeper's residence are all that remain. Some say it is the spirit of Fred Milliken, the lobsterman, that roams the station, banging doors and pulling down window shades. Others believe it's the restless, tortured soul of Howard Hobbs. Either way, visitors and volunteers at the lighthouse claim to feel that they're not alone at the place.

Sheri Poftak, historian for the group Friends of Wood Island Lighthouse, recently recounted a mysterious event that happened one weekend. "We have not been taking visitors up the tower" because it is too dangerous, she said. "There is a door in the lantern room which has been closed and the lighthouse locked except when we take tours in through the attached keeper's house. Well, I understand that as the last tour guide was leaving late [one] Sunday afternoon, she looked up and saw that the lantern-room door was open!"

According to Sheri, the door is virtually impossible to budge—unless, of course, you have the strength of a giant.

The first lighthouse at Wood Island was authorized by Thomas Jefferson and built in 1808. Essentially, it was a wooden tower primitive in comparison to later designs. It was constructed of a poor building material as well. By 1835, the tower had rotted so severely that a replacement was needed. The next lighthouse was forty-seven feet tall and constructed of granite rubble. It was operational by 1839. In 1858, the second tower was given an overhaul and upgraded with a fourth-order Fresnel lens. A bell tower was added in 1873 to assist mariners in finding their way during episodes of heavy fog.

Nearly a hundred years later, the traditional-looking lantern room was removed from the lighthouse and replaced with a more modern rotating beacon. Though it offered effective illumination of the surrounding sea and coastline, residents regretted that it looked nothing like the old light they remembered. They often complained that the "headless" tower needed to be returned to its former glory. In 1986, the Coast Guard returned the old-style lantern room to its proper place and automated the station with an optic called a VRB-25, thus ending the need for light keepers to physically man the tower, as had been done for well over a century and a half. The lighthouse is still an active aid to navigation. Its alternating green and white flashes can be seen for sixteen miles at sea.

Today, the Friends of Wood Island Lighthouse are overseeing the complete restoration and revival of the light station. For more information, call 207-284-1273 or visit www.woodislandlighthouse.org.

Access to Wood Island is limited. The island can be reached by private boat. Be careful, as a nasty variety of poison ivy plagues the area. The Friends of Wood Island Lighthouse offer tours departing from Vines Landing in Biddeford Pool. Check for times. The tour is free and takes approximately two hours. Donations to help toward further restoration are greatly appreciated. You'll be able to tour the house and peek inside the tower, but climbing the stairs is not yet possible.

For distant views of the lighthouse, try the trail along the shore of the Audubon Society property on East Point in Biddeford Pool. To reach the trail, follow ME 9/ME 208/Pool Road south from Biddeford Pool. After about five miles, turn left on ME 208. You'll arrive at an intersection. Turn left, then bear right, then bear right again onto Lester B. Orcutt Boulevard. Continue to East Point. The gate is on your left. Parking alongside the highway is allowed, although space is extremely limited at times.

THE ABIDING BRIDE

BOON ISLAND LIGHT
NEAR YORK, MAINE

"Now conscience wakes despair
That slumbered, wakes the bitter memory
Of what he was, what is, and what must be
Worse; of worse deeds worse sufferings must
ensue."

John Milton, *Paradise Lost*

Poet Celia Thaxter called Boon Island "the forlornest place that can be imagined." Eight miles off Maine's closest shore, it measures roughly seven hundred feet by three hundred feet and rises just fourteen feet above sea level. Overexposure to sun and brine, not to mention hurricane-strength winds and surf, have left the island devoid of vegetation and animal life. Jutting up from a dangerous shelf in the Atlantic Ocean, it is no more than a grim mound of craggy rock, treacherous enough to warrant a lighthouse but horrendously impractical to man. Though many tried to live there, the task proved humanly impossible. With few exceptions during the station's years of manned operation, light keepers vacated the post in a matter of weeks.

So hostile is the environment, in fact, that not even lighthouse towers could withstand the relentless pummeling of waves and wind. The first two lights erected on Boon Island were decimated by storms in 1804 and 1831. The prospect of ever building a structure durable enough to bear up under such tremendous forces seemed futile.

But in 1852, measures were taken to build a taller structure of solid granite blocks. It proved a wise decision. Since becoming operational on January 1, 1855, the current tower has stood rock-hard for over 150 years.

Standing 133 feet, Boon Island Light is the tallest lighthouse in New England. Though no longer manned, it continues to warn mariners to steer clear of its dangerous coast. Submerged nearby is a rocky ledge that has disemboweled countless unsuspecting vessels that ventured too close.

One of the most horrific events to happen at Boon Island took place on December 11, 1710, when the British ship *Nottingham Galley* wrecked, marooning its crew on the island for twenty-six days. The sailors resorted to eating their own. Local fishermen were so troubled by the disaster and the ensuing reports of cannibalism that they began leaving drums of rations on the island in case others should face similarly grim circumstances in the future.

This was the history of the island handed down to one young light keeper and his new bride, Katherine Brights, whose own experience there has become the stuff of legend.

As the story is told by old-timers, the couple arrived on the island in the mid- to late 1800s with prospects of a happy future together. Initially, all seemed to go well for the pair. Katherine had her sewing to idle away the long days, as well as the many books she intended to read as

Boon Island Light
© *2004 Bob and Sandra Shanklin, the "Lighthouse People"*

time allowed. And time seemed a commodity in no short supply as her husband looked after his many lighthouse duties—duties that, in due time, became a source of contention. Life on desolate Boon Island was not the sort of honeymoon Katherine had envisioned.

In the beginning, the isolation seemed somewhat romantic. Despite the landscape's austerity, Katherine liked the idea of being detached from the rest of the world, save for the two other keepers who helped man the light. She envisioned a simple life in a place of solitude where a common devotion to duty would bind her and her mate closer. They would prevail over the harsh environment, and be better for it. They would prove that, while nothing else could flourish on that barren rock, their undying love would. On calm nights when the beacon shone without worry, when both were weary from an honest day's work, Katherine fell asleep in her groom's arms. As long as they were together, life on the island would be paradise.

Even when, after a time, she longed for home so badly she would spend whole days puttering aimlessly, crying, and even screaming from boredom, all her frustration was assuaged come evening when a fire crackled in the front room and the house was filled with her husband's voice. One ordinary conversation a day, looking at him across the table, helping him clean the many glass prisms in the lantern room—such things wielded more power than all the forces of nature around them.

But when summer turned to fall and then winter, the storms grew stronger, with wind whipping across the island at record speeds and taking with it whatever wasn't battened down. The nights grew interminable. Katherine's conscientious young spouse was drawn away constantly, making repairs, oiling mechanisms, cleaning tools, maintaining various ledgers. *What on earth possessed a man with so many responsibilities to marry in the first place?* she began to wonder. He had become a ghost to her, appearing briefly, then vanishing with the howling wind.

One winter morning when the other keepers had rowed out to meet the tender—anchored at sea, away from the ledges—an unexpected storm blew in from the north. The young light keeper donned his oilskin and braved the arctic tempest that threatened to smash the island's remaining boat, the couple's only means of escaping the rock, should it become necessary. Waves soared high above the keeper's house, crashing down with the force of a furious sea monster. Katherine begged him not to strike out into the storm. It was too late, she argued. "You'll meet your death," she said. "Wait for the others to return."

But the light keeper knew that losing that boat meant calamity. "Don't worry. I'll be all right," he assured her. Then he kissed Katherine fiercely before grabbing a lantern and hastening into the storm.

For a while, she was able to follow his steps as he slogged through the sideways-blowing ice and rain toward the part of the island where the boat was tied. But within minutes, the fire from his lamp was snuffed by the storm. Katherine stoked the fire inside the keeper's house and hovered over its scant light and warmth. Outside, the wind and surf collided. She had heard stories about weather so violent on the island that the rocks were tossed until none was left unturned. And it was true, she discovered. It sounded as if the entire island was being ripped from its moorings and engulfed by the sea.

Throughout the darkening day, she prayed the storm would subside. When it didn't, she hoped that, at the very least, the other keepers would return to help search for her husband.

But hours passed and no one came. Finally, too panic-stricken to wait any longer, Katherine dressed herself as warmly as possible and took the first chance that presented itself. When the downpour tapered to a fine mist, she scrambled out after her helpmate, who by then had been gone all morning and afternoon. It was not more than ten minutes' distance across the whole island. He should have returned by now. Something dreadful must have happened.

And indeed it had.

When Katherine reached the spot where the boat had been secured, she could no longer feel her face. Ice caked her clothing, and her fingers prickled when she tried to bend them.

Her poor bridegroom was entombed in a thin casing of ice. She found him lying face down in the water, wedged between floating slabs of packed snow and the small boat, which also lay in ruin, smashed to fragments. She ran recklessly into the frigid water after him, clutching him to her body, sobbing hysterically, begging him to be all right—demanding it. "Don't you dare!" she wailed. Soaked through from the rain and now the battering surf, she howled with grief. For a short while, she stood in the water, teeth chattering, heart wrenching, staring tearfully out to sea, swaying back and forth with his body clenched tightly against hers. "Please," she begged. "Someone, help me!"

But she knew there was no one to heed her cries. She was utterly alone. The thought hit her like a clap of thunder, tearing through all sense of reason. She yelled despite herself, frantically, over and over, "Help! Can anyone hear me?"

But of course, no one could.

🕯

In life, her husband had been a smallish man who hadn't yet outgrown his attractive boyish features. He'd worn spectacles and a thin mustache.

She sank to the rocks and wept, wishing for nothing better than that she should drown as well. Then something caught her eye. There beside her were the thin spectacles of her husband. In their reflection, she saw clouds roiling above. The storm was regrouping.

Quickly, she scooped up the eyeglasses and tucked them inside a pocket. She must do something. She must think of a way to cart her bridegroom back to the keepers' house before nightfall.

A moment later, the clouds burst. Rain fell in blasts, the wind jerking it back up and around like a whip, so it lashed Katherine numerous times before striking the ground. There was no time to think and nothing nearby of any use. Only rocks. Everywhere, rocks! It was insane to think she could drag the body over the expanse of boulders that lay ahead of her, but she had no choice. An uncommon bolt of winter lightning crackled overhead, and Katherine yanked mightily on her husband's arm, freeing him from the ice and disentangling him from the length of rope he'd used to try and tie down the boat. He landed with a thud on the shore.

She made several futile attempts to tow him by his collar before she realized his clothing was compounding the problem. So she wrestled him out of his slicker and let it be dragged to sea. Then she pulled off his boots. They, too, bobbed away from the shore a short distance before filling with water and sinking.

When she was ready to try again, she lifted his legs with the intention of dragging him feet first. She pulled her husband's corpse behind her as if it were a sled. His body was rigid, his cold, bony feet pinned tightly under her arms.

She worked furiously in the storm, thankful she could not see how swollen he now was. She sensed it, though, in the outrageous burden his weight presented her. Time and again through the late evening, she questioned her good sense as she pulled his corpse, thumping against every rock, back to the keepers' house. She flinched with each blow delivered him, imagined the wounds she was inflicting, and felt a morbid sense of complicity in his cruel mistreatment. So strong was the feeling and so overcome by exhaustion was she that she nearly gave up. *Why not simply leave him and come back for him in the morning?* she asked herself in frustration. *What difference would it make?*

But quickly she scolded herself. Tears welled in her eyes at the thought of even a momentary lapse of her marital devotion. The prospect of having him tossed out to sea—of losing him so completely as that—was more than Katherine could stand to imagine.

Besides, she reasoned, even if he lasted through the night, she wasn't sure she would have the courage to approach him later, laid out there on the rocks. Right now, all that mattered was that he was still her husband, her life mate and one true love. But by morning, who knew what he would become?

So on she toiled until eventually, miraculously, she pulled his body inch by merciless inch across the vast space of ice and rocks to the safety of the lighthouse base. The keepers' residence appeared to Katherine too flimsy to withstand the storm—a storm that by then had fully regained its former strength, a storm so malevolent it simply would not die.

Closing the door behind her and pulling off the outer layer of her wet garments, Katherine reckoned the place was cursed. She shivered, either from the cold or from the chilling idea that something wicked meant to rid the island of every living creature. She wondered if even the lighthouse stood a chance. But waiting out the storm inside its walls—nine feet of granite at the base—was her only hope. There, she would pray for morning, pray for a break in the rain, pray for rescue.

Rescue!

It occurred to her that someone must man the light at all times, at all costs. She must not let it go out. She needed to sound the fog alarm and alter the flash pattern to make a clear distress signal that a passing ship would recognize.

Before she could catch her breath and warm herself, she searched for the matches stockpiled in the storage room below, and then the oil and the service manual. "Good, good," she said with each grateful discovery. She worked quickly, hurrying back to the vestibule with as much equipment as she could carry—logbooks, ammonia for cleaning the windows, fresh wicks.

Momentarily, she was distracted by the work. But then she found herself startled all over again by the sight of her husband lying in a lifeless heap on the floor at her feet. "Agh!" she said, dropping several of the articles she carried in her arms. She stood deathly still, waiting for something— though what, she could not say. Perhaps he would suddenly jerk back to life.

A chill ran through her bones, and she felt a queer sense of satisfaction. She smiled forlornly. For although her mate's spirit was lost to her, she had single-handedly salvaged his remains. When help arrived, they would take his body to the mainland for a proper Christian burial. She could look forward to that, at least.

Then a new whisper of terror rose inside her. What if the storm had taken the others as well, and no one should ever find her? What if their provisions had sunk to the bottom of the sea, along with the tender and all on board? The idea of being left without food or water reminded her of the grisly story of cannibalism among the crew of the *Nottingham Galley*. She shivered, then hastily waved the feeling away. *Nonsense,* she told herself. Surely, someone would see her signal. She bundled her supplies and wet clothes in a shawl, then grabbed the hem of her torn skirt. With the other hand, she took hold of the heavy oil can and, with much effort, slowly ascended the staircase. Someone would come. They must. And soon.

Winding her way up the 168 stairs to the lantern room on top, she was grateful to find the lamp still lit. "Oh, thank God," she said, gasping for breath, for life, for her own diminishing wits.

Then she set to work, first hanging her clothes to dry around the lantern room, then scouring the service manual for instructions on how to alter the fixed white light to one that flashed. When she found nothing, she thought of extinguishing and then relighting it at random intervals. Signals as erratic as those would certainly convey a crisis. Someone would sense her urgency. At least, she hoped they would.

After spending a great deal of time changing the strobe, she finally left it lit and kept a close watch for ships. But she found only mirages in the churning black water below. Ghost ships. Phantoms that vanished as quickly as they came into view. She began to wonder if she could trust herself. Already, her eyes grew weary. She could stand to look at the sea for only so long before it started to hypnotize her, play tricks on her. If she could hold out until morning, though, she was sure the weather would break and someone would come. But she feared that if she let the sea cast its spell upon her, she would fall into slumber and miss whatever chance she had of rescue.

For a time, she read the service manual, merely to keep herself occupied. When that grew tiresome, she busied herself with chores. She trimmed the wick and poured the can of oil into the furnace that powered the light. She scrubbed the windows with ammonia and wound the clockworks regularly, as required. By and by, though, she found herself sitting idle again.

And that's when the cold set in like a clammy hand. The temperature had fallen steadily through the night, but sometime during the early-morning hours, it bottomed out, rendering Katherine incapable of doing anything except shuddering with chills. As the garments hanging around the room dried, she pulled them back on. She even donned the cleaning coat she'd discovered in the storage room. Even so, she found herself growing increasingly cold. The furnace proved to be an insubstantial source of heat against the storm, for its fire was locked away deep inside the lantern mechanism and was no match for the wind that stole through the thin glass panes all around. Katherine hadn't even brought with her a hand lantern. The best she could do was strike a match every so often and thaw her fingertips over the tiny flame. But that was a drastic measure she took only when the cold became unbearable, for the matches were a precious commodity.

Finally, when she could bear it no longer, she descended the stairs in search of something to burn. Her husband had often built fires in the lantern room on cold nights with kindling provided by the Lighthouse Board, since none was available on the island. She would find it back at the keepers' quarters. She would also find food there. If the house seemed stable enough, maybe she would stay. She might build a fire in the hearth and keep a watch on the light from her bedroom window. Not having eaten in hours, she could almost taste the pilot bread and dried peaches she knew she'd find in the cupboard.

But as she descended halfway down the tower, she remembered that a corpse lay at the foot of the stairs. By now, she reasoned, it would have thawed completely. Skin she no longer remembered as ever being her husband's would have taken on a pasty dullness. Since he'd drowned, he would be swollen from taking on water. And even if that weren't the case, the corpse would surely have bloated from the due course of nature. Oh, how her thoughts decayed. She pictured a festering slab of mutton. The image so sickened her that she retched over the railing, then turned with a jerk and escaped up the stairs, where she bolted the lantern-room door.

Making its steady rotations, the beacon flashed like lightning, alarming her with each bright burst of illumination, then an eerie moment of darkness. With each strobe, she was blinded. But with each blackout, she saw shadows creep over the rocks, the dark silhouettes of menacing clouds roiling all around, the sea rising in waves that rushed toward her and ferociously broke against the tower somewhere below her view. With each lash, the tower moaned its suffering.

Hours passed in this manner—then days. When the sun rose, it was a worthless ice cube in the firmament. Katherine cursed it. "You," she shouted, pointing her finger, "what use have you?" She spat at the prized windows her husband had once spent hours scrubbing. In days, she hadn't slept, hadn't so much as nodded off. Instead, she'd sat tensely attuned to every creak, every slap of water, every squall of blustery weather. Even the rumblings of her own stomach frightened her.

She left the light burning day and night, for fear of not being able to relight it should the fire go out. It was a risk she considered carefully, taking into account how much oil she'd carried up earlier and how quickly she would need more.

Still, no one responded.

Finally, the light burned itself out, leaving Katherine without any hope of warmth or illumination. Now, truly, she began to freeze to death. All her energy had been expended trying to keep warm, and now her body would surely begin shutting down organs to protect the heart. The heart must be kept alive. The brain, too, although certain lobes would soon become superfluous. She felt it happening already.

But strangely, she soon began to feel warm again. Indeed, she started to perspire. She had developed a fever, and in her growing delirium, she pulled off layers of clothes and burned them with the matches one article at a time. Suddenly, all her senses were heightened. She could smell the sea corroding the mortar of the lighthouse. She could hear the mice working their way out of the storage room below, trying to get at the corpse, whose stench now permeated the closed-in air of the tower. "Hot!" she said in a voice she no longer recognized. Then, laughing wildly, she flung open the windows for air, and, oh, it was the elixir of life itself! *I must have more of it,* she thought, wrapping a white shawl—the last article of clothing she had—about her shoulders and running, almost tripping, down the stairs. It was no matter that a corpse awaited her. She had forgotten it completely.

When she encountered it, however, she ran to it, laughing. "Oh, dear," she said. "There you are." A concerned look crowded her features. "Are you all right?" She knelt to study the lifeless face. Then she gasped. "Oh, heavens!" she said. "You're not well. Why, you're cold as death. Stay here, my love. I'll fetch help."

Then she reeled out into the winter landscape, wearing only the thin white shawl. "Help!" she cried. "My husband isn't well." She wandered aimlessly around the island for hours, beseeching assistance. Sometimes, she faltered on the rocks and forgot what it was she was doing. But then she would remember and cry for help again. Her body felt insubstantial, as weightless and wispy as the fog of her breath. *Perhaps I've died,* she thought. Then she looked around in panic. *But why am I still here on these rocks? Am I to be damned to this crib of brimstone for eternity?*

But she had not died—at least not yet. Ultimately, rescue did arrive. A sword-boat captain found her wandering the island, looking gaunt from exhaustion, shock, and starvation. "My husband, my husband," was all she said. "He isn't well."

A few days later, still inconsolable, the young bride drew her last breath.

But fishermen say she still roams Boon Island. Wearing a thin white shawl, she is sometimes seen staggering pitifully over the boulders, bemoaning the loss of her groom, eternally beckoning ships to her rescue.

The last attempt to man the light at Boon Island came during a blizzard in February 1978, when floodwaters raged so violently that they pitched boulders into the keepers' quarters and the nearby buildings, destroying them for good. The keepers were forced to take refuge in the lantern room at the top of the lighthouse until they were rescued by helicopter the next day. As the storm reached its peak, blocks were ripped from the tower and pitched into the ocean.

Afterward, Coast Guard officials automated the station. In 1993, they replaced the second-order Fresnel lens with solar-powered optics. In 2000, the Fresnel lens was put on display at Kittery Historical and Naval Museum in the town of Kittery, just south of York.

Today, the island is uninhabited. Unless, of course, you count the ghost of Katherine Brights, a sad-faced young woman in white who old-timers say haunts this jagged strip of land, grieving the loss of her courageous spouse and—until the light was automated—helping man the station from beyond the grave.

In the early 1970s, Coast Guard keepers reported witnessing a number of strange events. One time, two Guardsmen were fishing from a boat that drifted out too far for them to return in time to light the station before dark. No one else was on the island. Yet right on time, they saw the light ignite in the tower. Another Coast Guard keeper reported that the station's Labrador retriever would occasionally chase something all around the island. Guardsmen never saw what the dog was after, but because of similar odd occurrences, they assumed it was a ghost. On other occasions, keepers heard doors opening and closing inexplicably and felt as if someone was watching them.

Leased to the American Lighthouse Foundation in May 2000, the Boon Island Light, listed on the National Register of Historic Places, is still an active aid to navigation. Though it is not open to the public, it is possible to see the light from the shores of York. Better views are afforded from private boats and local tour boats. For more information, contact the American Lighthouse Foundation in Wells by calling 207-646-0245. And be sure to visit the Museum of Lighthouse History, located at 2178 Post Road/US 1 in Wells. The museum is open daily in season and by appointment during the off-season. Admission is free, although donations are surely welcome.

Minot's Ledge Light
© *2004 Bob and Sandra Shanklin, the "Lighthouse People"*

The Portuguese Phantom

Minot's Ledge Light
Near Scituate, Massachusetts

> "Here was the new iron light-house, then unfin-
> ished, in the shape of an egg-shell painted red, and
> placed high on the iron pillars, like the ovum of a
> sea monster floating on the waves."
>
> Henry David Thoreau, *Cape Cod*

The first American lighthouse built in the open ocean
was Minot's Ledge Light, just outside Boston Harbor. The
submerged rock the beacon came to stand upon was such a
graveyard for vessels during the early nineteenth century that
something had to be done—and quickly.

Captain William Swift of the United States Army Topo-
graphical Corps was given the task of planning how a tower
might feasibly be built to withstand the full fury of the Atlantic. His contemporaries suggested modeling the lighthouse
after the famous Eddystone Light in the English Channel,
which was built in the shape of an oak tree but made of
stone rather than wood. Captain Swift favored an iron-pile

light, however, with a spidery, open framework that he was convinced would allow the elements to pass through, offering less resistance than a solid granite tower.

In the summer of 1847, a schooner housing workers was anchored nearby and construction got under way on the twenty-foot ledge. Operating on a budget of roughly thirty-nine thousand dollars, Swift planned for workers to drill a series of nine holes five feet deep into the rock, which would allow the iron tower to be secured directly onto the watery spit. Conditions at the site were so dangerous, however, that drilling could be performed only at low tide, when the ledge was dry for a few hours each day.

Working in twenty-minute shifts, groups of four men drilled from a platform built atop a triangular apparatus fixed to the rock by heavy spars. Every caution was taken, but even so, men and equipment were swept over the sides countless times during two terrific storms that summer. Thankfully, no one drowned.

But circumstances were so bad by the winter of 1847-48 that construction was halted until spring. It was September 1848 before iron pilings were successfully anchored into the ledge and capped by a cast-iron platform weighing five tons. The keepers' quarters and a sixteen-sided lantern room housing a Fresnel lens were erected on top.

It was an engineering feat unlike any other in the country. And had a last-minute change to the plans been avoided, the light might well have stood a hundred years. Some questioned the wisdom of omitting supports designed to reinforce the lower part of the tower. Perhaps those supports would have spared the lives of two assistant keepers whom many believe still man their posts on Minot's Ledge from the depths of their watery graves.

Ushering in the New Year and a new decade, keeper

Isaac Dunham first ignited the fixed light at Minot's Ledge on January 1, 1850. Mariners celebrated the beacon's guidance around the treacherous rock.

But after living at the light just a short while, Dunham was convinced the tower would never withstand a gale as severe as those reported in the area. In March 1850, he noted in his logbook that the structure reeled like a drunken man. "I hope God will in mercy still the raging sea," he added, "or we must perish. . . . God only knows what the end will be." According to some accounts, Dunham's cat was so frightened by the swaying of the tower that it jumped from the keepers' quarters to its death on the rocks below.

The keeper wrote to government officials requesting the addition of crossbeams to strengthen the structure, but his pleas went unheeded. When he could no longer stand the daily terror of his duties, keeper Dunham—along with his assistant, son Isaac A. Dunham—resigned. His tenure at Minot's Ledge was less than ten months.

Assuming command of the station in October 1850, John Bennett openly disparaged Dunham for his fears, suggesting the tower was as stable as could be wanted. Hoping to prove himself capable of his new post, the second keeper quickly hired two new assistants, Englishman Joseph Wilson and a Portuguese man named Joseph Antoine. The keeper informed his subordinates that no one should ever be left alone at the station. "Two men," he said, "shall remain at the light at all times."

"Aye," said Wilson.

"Understood," said Antoine in his lilting English.

An inspection of the braces revealed signs of strain, however, and within a few weeks of assuming his position, keeper Bennett changed his mind. It seems he concurred with Dunham after all. "Much remains to be done to secure it from accident," he reported.

On top of their regular duties, the new keepers had to

remove braces and ferry them to the mainland, where they were hammered straight again and strengthened, then brought back to the ledge and reattached to the lighthouse. Doubting the tower's stability must have weighed heavily on their minds. But as luck would have it, when a delegation arrived to look into the reports, the weather was dead calm, and the committee found no reason to take action.

That winter, however, an incredible storm sent mighty waves against the seventy-five-foot lighthouse, forcing the three keepers down from the lantern room to take refuge for four days and nights in the storage area below. Wind and water penetrated the windows overhead and repeatedly extinguished the beacon, leaving no choice but that someone had to relight it. Clinging desperately to the ladder outside, the men took turns climbing to make repairs. The tower bobbed like a buoy, thrashing the men so violently when they attempted the ascent that they were nearly shaken into the abyss below, where beneath the ledge there lived, according to Native Americans, an evil spirit called Hobomock.

Keeper Bennett must have feared the demon had been awakened, for before his turn of duty, he scrawled on a piece of paper, "Our situation is perilous. If anything happens before day dawns on us, we have no hope of escape." He rolled up the note and corked it inside a bottle he pitched into the sea as he mounted the ladder.

When the storm finally abated, Wilson and Antoine tightened the braces yet again.

In January 1851, Captain William Swift, the tower's architect, felt compelled to defend his design against critics who were looking at the lighthouse with increasing scrutiny. In a letter published in the *Boston Daily Advertiser*, he wrote, "Time, the great expounder of the truth or the fallacy of the question will decide for or against the Minot; but inasmuch as the light has outlived nearly three winters, there is some reason to hope that it may survive one or two more."

Tragically, it was not to be.

In April, easterly winds struck the coast with cosmic force. Keeper Bennett must have feared the braces would not withstand the tempest that threatened the tower. Though it's uncertain what happened in the final moments before his departure to the mainland, perhaps he urged Wilson and Antoine to help him repair the braces a final time. They must have worked furiously to remove the supports and send them with the keeper to be reinforced. All that's known for certain is that when Bennett attempted to return to the light station the following day, the storm was wreaking such havoc along the New England coast that it turned back any boat that tried to cross the water. Bennett watched helplessly as the lighthouse was battered by waves. All he could do was pray for the safety of his two assistants, left to man the light alone.

The brave actions of Wilson and Antoine probably saved the lives of countless seamen in the area during the great storm, for they continued to ring the bell and protect the light until the end. It is believed that around midnight on April 16, 1851, the Englishman and his Portuguese colleague wrote a final farewell to the world. Some sources say a bottle containing their fretful letter found its way to shore. Perhaps it spoke of how, like a giant sea devil, the storm splintered the iron pilings that held the great lantern room upright. Finally, the thirty-ton structure toppled over and smashed against the very rocks it had warned of. Perhaps one of the men courageously volunteered to face the storm head-on by climbing the ladder in those final moments to try and relight the lamp, while the other desperately hammered the fog bell.

All that's known for sure is what was officially reported: "The light on the Minot was last seen from Cohasset on

Wednesday night at ten o'clock. At one o'clock Thursday morning the light-house bell was heard on shore, one and one-half miles distant . . . and it was at this hour, it is generally believed, that the light-house was destroyed; at daylight nothing of it was visible from shore."

The body of assistant keeper Joseph Antoine washed ashore later at Nantasket. It is generally believed that his fellow serviceman, Joseph Wilson, survived long enough to reach nearby Gull Rock but died of exhaustion and exposure before he was discovered.

For the next nine years, lightships cautioned passing vessels of the danger posed by the shadowy tombstone of Minot's Ledge. Meanwhile, in 1855, construction began on a new lighthouse. General Joseph Totten of the Lighthouse Board designed the massive granite tower that stands today. Harking back to the solid design of Eddystone Light—as some had wanted to do from the start—the 114-foot structure combined a foundation bored and set directly into the ledge itself with a slanted tower intended to divert waves that threatened to topple it into the ocean. It cost $330,000 and took five years to finish, but the lighthouse has held up to every punishment the sea has put upon it—even waves that seem to swallow it whole—for the last 145 years.

Shortly after the 1860 tower became operational, mariners began reporting a phantom hanging from the bottom rung of the lighthouse ladder, as if clinging for dear life. Keepers, too, reported peculiar goings-on. Most often, they heard tapping sounds, which they attributed to the ghosts of the former assistants, who'd been known to signal each other in such a manner.

But other things happened as well. Sometimes, keepers made their rounds performing routine duties only to find that the lens had already been polished or the lantern had already been cleaned. Sometimes, they discovered the lamp had been filled when they were sure it needed oil. Inexplicably, no one ever acknowledged performing the chores. In time, the benevolent assistance was attributed to Wilson and Antoine, whom the new keepers believed had never left their posts at Minot's Ledge. Some even said they'd seen the pair above in the lantern room. And during calm seas, it was said that one could stare at the reflection of the lighthouse in the water and see what appeared to be the two drowned keepers standing in the doorway.

In 1947, the lighthouse was automated. The keepers were relieved of their solitary confinement on the rock, which had driven more than a few mad. Supposedly, one had threatened to kill the head keeper, and another went insane from living in a building without corners. According to an 1892 article in *Harper's Young People*, some even attempted suicide.

When the light was decommissioned, the Fresnel lens was removed and temporarily housed in one of the storage rooms below for safekeeping. Unfortunately, vandals broke into the tower and smashed several of the glass prisms before the lens could be transported to the Boston Museum of Science. Later, thieves attempted to steal the fog bell. Thankfully, their efforts were thwarted.

Today, visitors can see a replica of the lantern room housing the repaired Fresnel lens. In 1992, the Cohasset Lightkeepers Corporation raised money to restore the 1858 keeper's house at Government Island, across the harbor from Minot's Ledge. Herb Jason, a local fisherman, rescued the fog bell when it was about to be used for scrap. It is now on display as well.

In 2000, a granite monument dedicated to Joseph Antoine and Joseph Wilson was erected on Government Island. Locals will tell you their spirits still linger at Minot's Ledge. To this very day, people continue to sight the ghost of assistant keeper Joseph Antoine clinging to the bottom rung of the ladder outside the tower. His face is gaunt and filled with terror. If you're close enough, the story goes, you may even see the spectral figure wave one arm and hear him shout in his Portuguese accent, "Stay away! Stay away!"

Listed on the National Register of Historic Places, Minot's Ledge Light is located at Cohasset Rocks off Cohasset, Massachusetts. Though the lighthouse is inaccessible, you can see it from Government Island, where you can visit the keeper's quarters. But the light is best viewed by boat. For information about tours passing by Minot's Ledge Lighthouse, contact the Friends of the Boston Harbor Islands by calling 781-740-4290.

Today, the solar-powered lighthouse flashes a distinct pattern of 1-4-3, which has come to represent the number of letters in the phrase "I love you," earning the old sentinel its nickname, "the Lovers' Light."

The Curse of the Pirate Light Keeper

Bird Island Light
Marion, Massachusetts

"There was all the world and his wife."

Jonathan Swift, *Polite Conversation*

Like many New England lighthouse locations, Bird Island is a thin sliver of land, less than two acres, that calls attention to a cluster of hidden hazards—Bird Island Reef, as well as Centerboard Shoal in Sippican Harbor. In 1819, when the rubble-stone lighthouse was built on the island, the town of Marion was still part of Rochester, a shipbuilding settlement and a busy quay for whalers. The lighthouse tower was only twenty-nine feet tall, but thanks to its ten oil lamps and its pair of fourteen-inch reflectors, it was thought to be as powerful as the more impressive light at Gay Head, down the bay and across the sound on Martha's Vineyard.

The island was aptly named. Sometimes, the squawk of the many birds that came to nest in the tall grasses—fairy terns and noddies, mynahs and cardinals—was deafening. The first keeper at Bird Island was William Moore, who, according to legend, was banished to the remote location after being found guilty of piracy. Supplies were ferried to the island by the Lighthouse Service and by the villagers of Sippican, who were fond of the keeper's tobacco-loving wife. On their frequent trips to the island, they usually brought Mrs. Moore a little snuff or alcohol. Always, the old swashbuckler objected, asserting that his wife was stricken with consumption and needed to abstain from smoking her pipe, as she was wont to do. But because they pitied her, they went to great effort to slip her pouches of tobacco on the sly.

Mrs. Moore was not only in the habit of smoking a pipe but also of "taking" snuff—that is, inhaling it through the nostrils, as was common at the time. Pirate or not, Moore found the habit unbecoming a woman, especially his own wife. He considered the practice a sign of laziness.

And lazy he was not.

Though he appeared to some a crotchety old cuss, the truth of the matter was that William Moore was simply weary of the world. He sought refuge in the noble work of tending the lighthouse. As a former sailor, he esteemed more than most the lifesaving beacons all along the Atlantic that spared men a dreaded demise. And according to letters he wrote to the Massachusetts superintendent of lighthouses, he was actively seeking a way to keep whale oil from freezing during the coldest months of the year. After a hard life of piracy and privateering

Bird Island Light
© *2004 Bob and Sandra Shanklin, the "Lighthouse People"*

during the War of 1812—of raiding enemy ships and handing the spoils over to the government—William Moore had utterly transformed himself into a reliable lighthouse keeper.

His wife much preferred assisting her husband in maintaining the light to wasting away in some sanitarium choked with tubercular invalids. And if you believe the stories, the old pirate did care for his wife, in his odd, roguish way. Having survived untold conflicts with cutthroats, Moore didn't fear catching the disease himself. Some say he was even a gentle caretaker, wiping the corners of his watery-eyed wife's mouth when she coughed up blood or dabbing a cool handkerchief to her head on nights when she perspired so profusely it seemed the ocean spray had drenched their bedsheets.

According to tales, Mrs. Moore took great delight in seeing the villagers of Sippican. She relished their raucous merrymaking and pulled drams from their little brown jugs. Then she generously handed the potations round to others and danced to the fiddle playing.

The old pirate knew the health risks the missus was taking. "She suffers of contagious tuberculous," he told them, though they seemed not to heed his words of warning. Watching her drink the villagers' grog was difficult enough for Moore. But considering the implications of her passing the bottle, it completely unnerved him to think what would happen should an outbreak of consumption sweep the town of Sippican. The two of them would be banished from the island, from the lighthouse and its decent work—his last chance of redemption.

"No more," he said one evening. "I forbid your rum bibbing and cavorting. Don't you want a respectable life? Think of your own well-being. I mean it, daughter of joy. There'll be no more of it! No drink nor smoke. No tomfoolery, no turkey trot nor snuff taking. I'm tired of your larks. You're a wife, not a wench!"

The citizens of Sippican noted that, on more than one occasion, Mrs. Moore was badly bruised. Sometimes it was an arm, sometimes an eye. That was why they insisted on visiting as often as they could. They feared the keeper was abusive to the poor old wretch.

And indeed, as time passed, William Moore became the cruel oppressor they'd feared all along. He shut his wife up in the keeper's house for a time, out of reach of the villagers, whom he ran off when they came calling. "She ain't seeing visitors today," he told them. "She's not up to it, as I've been telling you these many months. She's a sick woman." The villagers of Sippican had no choice but to leave the island, for the keeper stood between them and the house. He watched until they climbed back in their boats and shoved off.

Meanwhile, William Moore fretted about his wife. He began to notice her diminishing interest in his experiments. No longer did she take delight in his retelling of the day's achievements or setbacks. "You and your wretched whale oil," she said, garnering a lash from the back of his hand, quickly tasting the blood of a split lip.

"I do this for your own welfare," he tried explaining, though it did no good.

Her spirit vanquished, she finally submitted to the disease. Her weight dropped dramatically, for she no longer had an appetite.

Unless you count tobacco.

She still craved her snuff, still longed for a taste of the villagers' home brew. Lacking their company, she grew so very tired. And in her stifling convalescence, her coughing redoubled. The sensation was one of being strangled by her own blood.

The old pirate withdrew more and more often to one of the sheds, where he labored over his research. No one knows how long he locked himself away from his wife, leaving her alone in the house to tend to her own needs—or else to die. But legend holds that when he returned to the keeper's residence one cold February morning in 1832, he found her astonishingly spirited once again. She had made her way from her sickbed to the porch, the first time in weeks.

"Aye, God!" the old pirate said when he saw her. "What witchcraft is this?" Although she didn't respond, some familiar twinkle in her eye set the cogs in his brain a-turning. She rose to step off the porch into the blanket of snow covering the island, a blast of arctic wind hitting her in the face. "Where is it?" Moore bellowed. "I smell it on your rotten breath, tart! They've come again, ain't they?"

Mrs. Moore was too boozy to answer. Down the stairs she went, grasping the handrail and overcompensating for the wobble in her walk. Gingerly, gingerly, she picked her way across the yard, leaving Moore slack-jawed and outraged back at the house.

"Damn you, woman!" he cursed. "Damn ya to hell!" Then, in a final fit of frustration, he lunged inside, claimed the old blunderbuss he'd put away, and chased down his wife in the falling snow. The shots were never heard across the harbor. Mrs. Moore's diseased blood soaked through the crisp white snow and leached into the cold earth beneath.

Responding to distress signals the old pirate issued from the island, the townspeople found Moore awaiting their arrival alone. By then, his wife was dead. Blood was everywhere, though her husband insisted she had "succumbed from nicotine." After convincing the would-be rescuers his wife truly had suffered from contagious tuberculous, Moore buried her, with the help of his neighbors, in the loose sand on the beach. By the time the villagers' skepticism prompted them to report the suspicious death to the sheriff, William Moore had gone missing, never to return.

Some fifty years later, when the original keeper's house

was demolished in 1890, a gun was discovered stashed with a bag of tobacco and a damning letter signed by Moore. "This bag contains tobacco, found among the clothes of my wife after her decease," the letter stated, according to Edmund Tripp, town historian of Marion. "It was furnished by certain individuals in and about Sippican. May the curse of the High Heaven rest upon the heads of those who destroyed the peace of my family and the health and happiness of a wife whom I Dearly Loved."

It remains a mystery if William Moore's curse is to blame for the string of bizarre mishaps that beset the island. But there are those who believe a hex has driven people away since his disappearance.

The brother of Charles Clark, Jr., lighthouse keeper at Bird Island in 1890 when Moore's letter was found, accidentally shot himself while cleaning a gun. His brother's brush with death was the final straw for Clark, whose family had complained for years that the lighthouse was plagued with a number of problems. He and his relatives left soon afterward.

Then, after Peter Murray assumed the post at Bird Island, the new keeper's eleven-month-old son fell deathly ill with pneumonia. When the doctor summoned by Murray's distress signal attempted to cross the harbor to tend the ailing child, a tremendous storm blew in, forming ice floes so dense he was unable to make the trip. The toddler died and was buried back on the mainland, where the Murrays returned, never to set foot on Bird Island again.

Finally, what's known as "the Great Hurricane of 1938" ripped over the isle, stripping it of all buildings except the simply made rubble-stone tower itself. Was the curse of William Moore responsible for rendering the station uninhabitable?

According to legend, Mrs. Moore's spirit has roamed restlessly over the last century and a half. Later lighthouse keepers were vexed by her ghost—an old crone, they said, with a dreadful crook in her spine. Reportedly, she woke one keeper and his wife so often by rapping on the door in the middle of the night that the pair couldn't contend with it. Given that they were the only people on the island, the couple surmised it was a phantom. They left for the mainland soon afterward. Other keepers claimed their children were frightened by the spectral figure of an old lady, ugly and humpbacked. And in the early 1980s, two local fishermen reported seeing a crippled, rumpled-looking old woman smoking a pipe. She seemed to float just inches above the ice floes in the harbor as she made her way to the island.

No one knows the fate of William Moore, though some believe he returned to the high seas, more ruthless than ever. It's something you might think about should you ever sail near the island teeming with birds. And if you happen to see an old woman bony faced and bruised, shoulders twisted by age, fear not. It is only the wayward spirit of Mrs. Moore, ever searching for the villagers of Sippican and their generous offerings of tobacco and rum.

In 1994, Charles Bradley founded the Bird Island Preservation Society, whose efforts to restore the historic lighthouse called upon the expertise of the International Chimney Corporation. Thanks to funds from a federal grant, private donations, and a three-thousand-dollar contribution from the Marion Board of Selectmen, the group renovated the tower and installed a new solar-powered optic. The Bird Island Lighthouse was relit in a ceremony on July 4, 1997.

For a distant view of the lighthouse, turn left off Front Street/MA 105 in Marion onto US 6/Wareham Road, take the next right onto Creek Road, then take another right onto Point Road. From there, drive toward the entrance to Kittansett Club, a private golf course, and look across the bay. For even better views, charter a boat. For more information about the lighthouse, contact the Bird Island Light Preservation Society by calling 508-748-0550.

New London Ledge Light
© *2004 Bob and Sandra Shanklin, the "Lighthouse People"*

YEARNING ERNIE

NEW LONDON LEDGE LIGHT
NEW LONDON, CONNECTICUT

"Sweet is true love tho' given in vain, in vain;
And sweet is death who puts an end to pain."

Alfred, Lord Tennyson, *Idylls of the King*

Surrounded by water in New London Harbor, the ledge light looks more like the famed house in Alfred Hitchcock's *Psycho* than a navigational beacon. Built in the French Second Empire style, it rises surreally from the sound, three stories high with a mansard roof and all the gilding and trim of a haunted mansion. Curiously, some say that's just what it is.

Strange things have happened here since the light's construction in 1909. People have heard disembodied voices, foreign footsteps, eerie scraping sounds, and other peculiar bumps in the night. Some have smelled dead fish as if a cloud of odor had suddenly settled around them, while others have felt cold spots that couldn't be attributed to drafts. Curators have been startled by unexplainable blasts from the foghorn, by lights flickering off and on, by doors opening and closing of their own accord. One Coast Guardsman told of cups inching across a table and a radio that, when moved from its location in a certain area of the fourteen-room structure, would mysteriously find its way back.

Locals have taken to calling the entity residing in the lighthouse Ernie, though in 1981 a medium brought in to communicate with the ghost said its name was John Randolf. Although the presence never makes itself visible to men, women and children living in the house have seen it—the spectral figure of someone standing at the foot of their beds, a tall, bearded man wearing an oilskin slicker and rain bibs.

Ask New Londoners about Ernie and they'll tell you he was once a keeper at the New London Ledge Lighthouse. Some say that when he came to the area, he brought with him a wife younger by half than himself. She was a pretty little thing—named Rose, if an old town's memory can be trusted. It was the Roaring Twenties, when girls took to wearing shorter hairstyles and hemlines and started smoking cigarettes, rolling down their stockings, and powdering their knees. Rose didn't smoke cigarettes, but she did sport a modern, short bob dyed shockingly yellow but attractive nonetheless.

Still, it was odd picturing her a light keeper's wife. Now and then, the two of them rowed over to New London for supplies. She looked like a child with old Ernie, running ahead of him down the wharf, pouting when he said she couldn't take home one of the alley cats that hung around yowling for fish parts. "Ah, applesauce, Ernie," she'd say. "Sometimes, you're a real flat tire."

The townspeople said she looked like a girl easily bored. And they were right.

Ernie wanted children—especially a daughter with her mother's sea-green eyes and mischievous grin. A child who would have the run of the house. He could see Kewpie dolls and whirligigs on the staircase, *The Adventures of Poor Mrs. Quack* open faced on the front-room rug. Before the child could walk, Ernie wanted to take her up to the cast-iron lantern room mounted atop the center of the house. Like anyone else, the child would marvel at the three white flashes followed by a burst of red. Pointing to the coast, Ernie would say, "There's New London. See all the pretty houses? Ours was made to fit in amongst them. But it cost $93,968 to build, though." Then he'd whistle for emphasis and say, "That's a lot of simoleons."

To himself, he thought how lucky he was that New London Ledge still needed him to man the light. Electricity was reducing the number of keepers required by the Lighthouse Board, and someday soon, he knew, the work would end.

But there was no child, not yet. It was only the two of them. Rose, beautiful girl, how she bewitched him! She was into Freud and personality typing. It was a sort of game she played. At first, she calculated the behaviors of celebrities, based on forty questions. She was a great fan of jazz, listened to the radio day and night—the moans and growls of Bessie Smith, Gershwin's big symphony scores, Duke Ellington's "Sophisticated Lady." She had calculated all their personalities. Gershwin was a sheik, Ellington the real McCoy, Bessie Smith a hotsy-totsy.

Going about his chores at the lighthouse, Ernie listened to Rose's psychoanalysis with contentment. Everything about her made him feel lighter inside. She spoke of the subconscious and repression. People were complex, she said, even Ernie. When she analyzed him, she said, "You're a push-over, a sap!" Then she laughed and said, "I'm only razzing you."

Ernie bristled momentarily, though he continued to smile a bleak, tight-lipped half-smile. She was young, and it was important she thought him a good sport.

She seemed to study his face each time she spoke. This time, just as his smile began to pull into a sour grin, she spoke again: "You have an oral personality. But it's okay, see, 'cause I do, too."

Then they drank a toast from a small flask of bootleg whiskey Ernie had been saving.

"Only difference between us, Ernie, is that all I know is passive enjoyment." She took a swig from the flask and looked at him with an expression of faint amusement. "I was conditioned from childhood to keep an eye out for an easy source of entertainment." She raised the flask again, this time unsmiling.

For a while, Rose had luck convincing Ernie to take her into town for some action. It hadn't taken long for the novelty of the lighthouse to wear off. Rose wanted a little excitement—a speakeasy, a dance marathon, anything just so long as there was jazz and a good crowd.

But when Ernie had to stay home and tend the light, Rose paced the floor and turned the radio up to full volume. "Stupid boat," she'd curse. "Stupid water. Stupid, stupid lighthouse."

Then one day, she told Ernie she was going to take a ferry ride over to Block Island. She'd seen everything there was in New London. Ernie felt sure it was the last he'd see of her, that she'd ride into New York and never come home. But when the Block Island ferry returned that evening, Rose was on it. She came bounding down the gangway, the captain holding out a hand to help her step off the boat and onto the fifty-foot concrete pier supporting the lighthouse and hiding the dangerous ledge and the brackish water below.

The next day, she took another ferry ride out to the island.

"Well, what did you think of it?" Ernie asked afterward.

"Think of what?"

"Block Island."

"Oh, you know. It was okay and all."

But the following day, after taking another ride on the ferry, Rose admitted she hadn't yet actually visited the island, though she meant to on her next trip. Ernie had his suspicions, as any husband would. But when one day she didn't return—not even after a week, nor after two—and then the news came that she'd run off with the captain of the Block Island ferry, well, old Ernie was in sad shape. Everyone else saw it was coming, but for some reason, he hadn't.

The story goes that, once he was sure she'd left him for good, Ernie grieved for Rose. He began acting peculiar, cleaning the house with fits of energy, polishing the brass, swabbing the deck covering the massive pier. Then he suddenly became despondent and let his chores go unfinished. No one knows for sure how low his spirits sank in those final days, only that he was gripped with a despair that eventually made him take his own life. According to legend, after Rose ran off with the Block Island ferry captain, Ernie slit his throat and tossed himself over the railing of the lighthouse into the cold waters of the Atlantic.

Afterward, stories circulated that Ernie's spirit remained alive and well at the ledge light. According to Coast Guardsmen later stationed there, Ernie was sometimes heard tinkering in the lighthouse. Some swore he swabbed the decks in the wee hours of the morning. Others who found open paint cans with brushes inside firmly believed that Ernie was planning to paint the lighthouse.

Others weren't so easily convinced. Some local fishermen scoffed when the subject of Ernie came up. But it was the prankster Ernie who had the last laugh. The skeptics found their boats, previously tied securely to the pier, mysteriously set adrift.

The New London Ledge Light calls attention to a dangerous underwater ledge and a long shoal that extends from it. Although another lighthouse already stood in New London Harbor, its light proved insufficient for guiding vessels around the ledge marking the entrance to the port. Construction on the new lighthouse began in 1906 and concluded in 1909. Resting on a riprap crib eighty-two feet square and ten feet thick, the New London Ledge Lighthouse was designed to blend in with the architecture of the grand homes along the New London coast. Ironically, the hurricane of 1938 later destroyed many of those homes. Sporting a fourth-order Fresnel lens, the lighthouse cast an incandescent beam visible eighteen miles away. Today, it boasts a solar-powered optic. Listed on the National Register of Historic Places, the light is currently leased by the New London Ledge Lighthouse Foundation, whose efforts to restore it continue.

Tours of the lighthouse are offered through the University of Connecticut. For information, call Project Oceanology at the Avery Point Campus in Groton at 800-364-8472 or visit www.oceanology.org. To reach Project Oceanology from I-95, take Exit 87 and follow CT 349/Clarence B. Sharp Highway. At the second traffic light, turn right on Rainville Avenue. At the next light, turn left on Benham Road. Drive to the second entrance of the Avery Point Campus, continue toward the water, and park in front of the Project Oceanology building.

Ferry rides are also available. For information, call the Block Island Ferry at 203-442-7891.

Distant views of the New London Ledge Lighthouse are possible from Eastern Point Park. In Groton, take CT 349/Chester Street south toward Eastern Point Road. Take a sharp right off CT 349 onto Beach Pond Road, then bear left on Rita Santa Croce Drive to enter Eastern Point Park. At certain times, access to the park is restricted to residents of Groton. If you're turned away, drive up Shore Avenue, where you'll find another beach nearby on your left.

Point Lookout Light
© *2004 Bob and Sandra Shanklin, the "Lighthouse People"*

AMERICA'S MOST HAUNTED LIGHTHOUSE

POINT LOOKOUT LIGHT
CHESAPEAKE BAY, MARYLAND

"The Minstrel Boy to the war is gone
In the ranks of death you'll find him,
His father's sword he has girded on,
And his wild harp slung behind him."

Thomas Moore, "The Minstrel Boy"

Once a year, the chains come off the gated fence surrounding Point Lookout Lighthouse, purportedly America's most haunted, to allow visitors a chance to witness for themselves the reasons for this place's notoriety. Following the Ghost Walk, held in the town each Halloween, the duplex-style lighthouse is opened for one or two days, usually around the first week in November. Tour guides relate the strange goings-on in the kitchen, speak of the numerous ghostly voices caught on tape, and point to the landing at the top of the stairs where Ann Davis, a former keeper, appears wearing a white blouse and a long, blue skirt.

To some, Point Lookout is merely a state park made up of 1,046 acres of prime recreational real estate where fishermen bait lines and wait patiently, where cyclists pedal the park roads, and where outdoorsmen pitch tents in the 143 campsites.

But vacationers aren't the only people drawn here. Located at the confluence of the Potomac River and Chesapeake Bay, Point Lookout also appeals to history buffs. More specifically, it calls to Civil War enthusiasts. For although it's true that the area was first explored in 1612 by Captain John Smith, and that in 1648 colonists settling the area were massacred by Indians from nearby Virginia, and that it's been the site of numerous shipwrecks over the years, what most attracts historians to Point Lookout is Camp Hoffman.

During the Civil War, a sprawling military hospital was built at Point Lookout with annexes radiating from it like arms on a starfish. The wards filled quickly with wounded Union soldiers and later a small number of Confederate prisoners of war. After the Battle of Gettysburg, Hammond Hospital, as it was named, was enlarged, and Camp Hoffman, a prison camp, was established at the barren tip of the peninsula near the 1830 lighthouse.

Surrounded by water on three sides, the camp was difficult to escape. Only fifty people are believed to have ever succeeded. Most didn't even try. The government, therefore, saw little reason to construct any facilities to house its enemies. Instead, the prison consisted simply of two expansive pens—one about thirty acres in size, the other about ten acres—barricaded by a fence fifteen feet high and watched over by Union troops who fired down into the pens at anyone who crossed the boundary inside.

Of the fifty-two thousand prisoners of war incarcerated

at Camp Hoffman, at least thirty-three hundred perished from exposure, starvation, or pestilence. Descendants of the camp's internees actually put the number closer to fourteen thousand, suggesting the first figure accounts only for those buried in the cemetery at Point Lookout.

All agree, though, that the camp was hell on earth. Men chased down rats and seabirds and devoured them raw. Those who didn't starve to death were weakened or killed by scurvy. They were lice-ridden and exposed to filth and infectious diseases. Less than a thousand discarded Union tents were handed out to more than nine times that many prisoners, and blankets were distributed one to every sixteen men. In winter, the prisoners braved snow and ice without coats or even shoes. And in summer, they risked catching malaria, typhoid fever, and smallpox due in part to the dirty standing water and flood-plain sludge that resulted from the pens' location only five feet above sea level. It was the largest detention center of its kind. Many say the atrocities that occurred there between 1863 and 1865 account for the multitude of paranormal activities plaguing the whole point, not the least of which occur in the derelict old lighthouse.

Built in 1830 by John Donahoo, the original keeper's dwelling was a four-room brick structure. It was manned by James Davis, who took office in September of that year. But since the building was only one story tall, and since the lantern rose through the roof, the lamp was barely twenty-four feet off the ground and offered little aid to mariners in the bay.

In the 1850s, the old rotating lamps and reflectors were upgraded with a fourth-order Fresnel lens. In 1872, a fog bell added further assistance. But it wasn't until 1883—some records say the 1920s—that the house was expanded to a two-story duplex and the light was lifted seventeen feet higher. It was then that the lighthouse really became useful.

Keeper Davis's tenure at Point Lookout was short lived.

He held his post for only a few months before dying on December 3, 1830. Upon his death, Ann Davis assumed his responsibilities. She remained at the lighthouse until her own death in 1847. There are those who contend she mans the light still, for she is believed to be one of the spirits dwelling in the house today. On occasion, she is said to show herself to visitors and residents. Usually, she's seen standing at the top of the staircase.

Another female keeper at Point Lookout is rumored to have been a Rebel sympathizer during the Civil War. Some think she even harbored prisoners in the lighthouse. Pamelia Edwards's father, Richard Edwards, was assigned to the lighthouse in 1853. But he, too, died after only a few months at his duties. Pamelia's older sister Martha assumed their father's responsibilities for nearly two years. It's believed that Martha resigned when she became engaged, after which the role fell to Pamelia, who may have solicited her brother Elkannah to be her assistant. Pamelia remained at the lighthouse for fourteen years. Rumors circulated that she was removed from her duties in June 1869 for her involvement with prisoners during the war. Pamelia may be the reason some psychics have said they believe prisoners were once in the house.

The lighthouse was decommissioned in 1966. Civilian residents who moved in later told of all sorts of weird things happening in and around the station.

One such resident was Gerald Sword, a former park manager of Point Lookout. Gerald lived in the north side of the lighthouse in the late 1970s. He reported that he once saw the kitchen wall suddenly start to glow. The glowing persisted for about ten minutes. He also heard what sounded like someone snoring in the kitchen, a phenomenon that occurred every night for two weeks. During storms, Gerald heard people talking both inside and outside the house, and he frequently heard someone walking up and down the stairs and the hallway. He heard doors slam, saw lights go off and on, and smelled a foul odor in the living room. But the most inexplicable thing he witnessed happened on the anniversary of the sinking of the steamer *Express*. In 1989, Gerald wrote this account: "Among the more exciting events was the three dimensional appearance of a clean-shaven white male, wearing a sack coat and a floppy-brimmed hat. He arrived at the Cornfield Harbor side of the lighthouse just as a sudden and violent electrical storm whipped across the Potomac from Virginia. As this writer opened the door to the lighthouse to welcome him in from the approaching storm, he floated—yes, floated— right through the wire of the screened porch and never said a word nor left a trace.

"About 15 minutes later, the storm had passed. At that time, the door to the lighthouse slammed shut with great force. But the door was locked with the deadbolt just as I had left it 15 minutes earlier after my guest floated through the screened door. Several years later, I learned that 100 years before, almost to the day, the steamship *Express* had broken up off the point during a hurricane and many of the crew and passengers drowned. One of the crew was a white male from Baltimore, aged 24 years. It was his job to look for the Point Lookout Light so that the steamer could get around the point into Cornfield Harbor. The man's body washed up on the beach several days later, wearing a sack coat. He was buried nearby."

Laura Berg was the last person to inhabit the lighthouse. Although she never actually saw a ghost during the few years she lived there, she often felt as if someone was watching her whenever she descended the stairs. One of the most convincing pieces of evidence of ghosts at Point Lookout was captured during Laura's stay at the lighthouse. She was present when a photograph was taken that later revealed what seemed to be a ghost in the background. In 1980, a medium from the Maryland Committee for Psychical

Research was brought in to investigate the lighthouse. Her name was Nancy Stallings. The photo was taken of Nancy standing alone in one of the house's bedrooms. But the developed picture clearly revealed someone else in the room. Leaning against the wall behind Nancy, the figure appeared to be a man dressed like a Confederate soldier. Laura siad there was no other person present when the photo was snapped.

Another group of investigators who studied the house during the time Laura resided there discovered and recorded over twenty-five different voices inside the lighthouse. When their work was concluded, Dr. Hans Holzer, the team leader, turned to Laura and said, "This place is haunted as hell."

In October 1999, two college students helping with the Ghost Walk were flipping the lights inside the lighthouse off and on to make the place appear spookier to visitors. Everyone else was outside. Though the students didn't hear anything out of the ordinary, they told other Ghost Walk staffers that they felt uncomfortable inside the house. A tape recorder running at the time caught the ominous voice of an angry male saying, "Get out or perish!"

The following October, three adults were hoping to catch voices on tape again. Lucky them—they did. This time, what they captured was, "You don't belong here. Get out of my house!"

Other snippets caught on tape include, "Young man, danger everywhere" and "I have to face them."

Laura Berg and an assortment of volunteers have heard whistling, drumming, and chanting inside the station. No wonder Point Lookout Lighthouse is thought to be the country's most haunted!

In 1981, the navy told Laura Berg it could no longer rent the lighthouse to civilians. She was forced out, and the property soon became the target of vandalism. Later, after Laura visited the station in the 1990s and was disturbed by its dilapidated condition, she began a campaign to restore it. Through her perseverance, the run-down lighthouse is now on the National Register of Historic Places and on its way to recovery.

Laura Berg continues her efforts to preserve the place she once called home. In 2000, she and fellow lighthouse advocate Robert Hall developed the website www.ptlookoutlighthouse.com with hopes of reviving interest in the project. For more information, visit the website or call the Maryland Park Service at 301-872-5688.

On July 1, 2002, the state of Maryland purchased Point Lookout Lighthouse, which it hopes to eventually turn into a museum.

To reach Point Lookout Lighthouse from the community of Scotland, take MD 5 south to Point Lookout State Park, then continue two miles to the lighthouse at the end of the road.

Currituck Beach Light
© *2004 by Sheryl Monks*

The North Room

Currituck Beach Light
Corolla, North Carolina

"Grief fills the room up of my absent child,
Lies in his bed, walks up and down with me."

William Shakespeare, *King John*

The last major lighthouse built on North Carolina's treacherous Outer Banks was the 162-foot-tall red-brick Currituck Beach Light in 1875. Until then, one final stretch of coastline between Virginia's Cape Henry Light and North Carolina's Bodie Island Light remained unlit. One million bricks were used to construct the soaring tower, which housed a first-order Fresnel lens. Its light could be seen eighteen miles out to sea.

Shortly after the light was completed, the Lighthouse Board shipped precut materials to the site for the construction of a Victorian stick-built keepers' house. Though the house appears to be one large residence, it is actually a duplex that accommodated the primary keeper and his family on one side and additional keepers and their families on the other. Until the smaller keeper's house located on the premises today was moved from another site in the 1920s, the assistant keepers could expect a crowded arrangement. At one time, assistant keeper William Riley Austin shared half of the duplex with his brother Wesley and both of their families—nineteen people altogether. Under the circumstances, it's easy to imagine how difficult it must have been for the assistant keepers' wives to look after all those children, and how one might stray from time to time. Sadly, that's what happened one summer.

Today, the grounds are surrounded by lofty pines and lush weeping willows whose leaves sway in the coastal breeze. But in 1891, when assistant keeper William Riley Austin was transferred from the screw-pile lighthouse at Hatteras Inlet to Currituck Light, the views were completely unobstructed on both sides of the island—out across the sound on one side and as far as the eye could see into the Atlantic Ocean on the other. The entire area was wind-swept, the sand supporting only the most minimal of vegetation. What little did exist was foraged by the Banker ponies that ran wild over the islands.

By the second decade of the new century, William and his wife, Louise, had seven children, among them a young daughter who was continually drawn to the water's edge, where she loved to build sand castles. Lovie, as Louise was known, could scarcely undertake any kind of chore around the light station without having to cease work and go in search of the curly-haired girl. Though she cautioned the child never to venture toward Currituck Sound without the company of one of her older siblings or cousins, Lovie looked up from her work time and again to find the venturesome girl missing from the huddle of children playing nearby. No manner of punishment or strict warnings could frighten her. Nearly each day, she carried an old bucket down to the beach and began constructing a new sand castle, always grander than the previous day's.

One day, Lovie was overburdened with chores and sent an older child to the sound to fetch the young beachgoer. "She won't come," the messenger reported. Sometime later, Lovie sent an even older child whose authority the headstrong girl would not refuse. But again, the messenger returned alone. By that point, Lovie had had enough. She went to retrieve the girl herself.

Lovie took off her shoes and made her way through the sand where the little girl liked best to play. But the child was nowhere in sight. She tried another spot the girl frequented, but again there was no trace of her. Growing frantic, Lovie searched the beach in both directions. Finally, she solicited the help of the rest of the family. They searched all through the night, but the girl was not to be found.

Tragically, a day later, the child's body surfaced in the bay and was retrieved by a crew of local fishermen. The entire Austin family was overcome with grief, but Lovie was inconsolable. She locked herself away in her bedroom, the north room, and grieved for the girl. She mourned all day, and if she slept at all at night, she was shaken awake by dreams that left her crying till morning. Her health declined so drastically over the next few months that an old friend from Kitty Hawk was called upon to come and spend time with her. Little was it known, however, that Lovie's friend was herself stricken with some strange illness. During her stay at the lighthouse, she passed away, and her body was sent back home for interment.

Following that, Lovie was diagnosed with tuberculosis and was quarantined in her room. For his safety, William was forced to move into another room with some of the young males of the family, making conditions even more cramped in the assistant keepers' half of the duplex. As her illness progressed, Lovie fell into a state of deep despair. In her delirium, she called to her dead child. But of course, the girl could not come to her mother's bedside, nor could any of the other children, for they were strictly forbidden. Eventually, the poor woman died.

Afterward, all of her belongings were locked away in a wooden trunk and sealed inside the north room next to her deathbed. Tuberculosis was fatally contagious, and everyone in the house feared contracting it from articles with which Lovie might have come in contact.

William Riley Austin retired from his post at the Currituck Beach Lighthouse in 1929, and the Coast Guard abandoned the station altogether in the late 1930s. But for years afterward, villagers cautioned their children never to let their curiosity get the best of them. "Stay away from the lighthouse," they warned. "And for heaven's sake, keep out of the north room."

Of course, kids will be kids, and you can guess what happened. Eventually, a group of youngsters sneaked into the keepers' residence, went in search of Lovie's old trunk, pried it open, and scattered her most private possessions all about. When the worried townsfolk caught wind of the incident, they set the trunk and all it contained ablaze.

After that, the house was left untended until it fell into disrepair. In the late 1970s, Currituck County officials asked the North Carolina Wildlife Resources Commission to burn the station. Luckily, a group of concerned citizens stepped in to save both keepers' residences, the lighthouse tower, and all the station's ancillary buildings. Headed by John Wilson, a young graduate student studying historic preservation, the nonprofit group Outer Banks Conservationists was formed and came to the station's rescue. Since that fateful day, the Currituck Beach Lighthouse has been almost totally overhauled. Today, it draws as many as a hundred thousand visitors a year to its impeccably maintained premises.

But according to curators, some people have refused to enter the north room, where Lovie Austin died. Some have claimed they felt a strong presence inside the room, an unsettling anguish that filled them so dreadfully with despair that they couldn't stand to remain inside. And though visitors still occasionally stay at the house, no one has ever had the courage to share the room with Lovie's grief-stricken ghost.

The Currituck Beach Lighthouse was listed on the National Register of Historic Places in 1973. To reach it, take US 158 through Jarvisburg. At Point Harbor, US 158 crosses Currituck Sound and then runs into NC 12. Take NC 12 north toward Duck and Corolla. The lighthouse is twenty miles from the junction of US 158 and NC 12. Look for the Whalehead Club sign. The lighthouse entrance is on the left just beyond the sign.

The lighthouse and the museum shop are open daily from Easter to the day before Thanksgiving. For more information, call Outer Banks Conservationists, Inc., at 252-453-4939 or visit the lighthouse's website at www.currituckbeachlight.com. To reach the keepers, call 252-453-8152.

Cape Hatteras Light
© 2004 by Sheryl Monks

The Disappearance

of Theodosia

Cape Hatteras Light
Buxton, North Carolina

> "Such souls,
> Whose sudden visitations daze the world,
> Vanish like lightning, but they leave behind
> A voice that in the distance far away
> Wakens the slumbering ages."
>
> Sir Henry Taylor, "Philip Van Artevelde"

The Gulf Stream, flowing north from the Gulf of Mexico, has long carried mariners from that region of the Americas to the cities of the northern United States and on to Europe, while the southbound Labrador Current has pulled vessels in the opposite direction. These sailing lanes make the waters along the East Coast one of the most traveled arteries of the open sea. But at Cape Hatteras, North Carolina, the two currents collide, and boats are forced into the narrow channels and submerged rocks of Diamond Shoals. Here, shifting sand bars have claimed hundreds of vessels, earning the area its menacing nickname, "the Graveyard of the Atlantic." Lacking any prominent natural markers, sailors often were forced to hug the shoreline as they warily maneuvered through the fog hastened by the overlapping of warm and cold waters.

One of the earliest proponents of a lighthouse at Cape Hatteras was Alexander Hamilton, who as a young man was aboard a ship that got caught in a terrible storm there. For twelve hours, all on board the *Thunderbolt* fought to keep the ship from being splintered by the sea and to extinguish a fire that started in the galley as a result of the storm. The soon-to-be statesman vowed that, should he ever have the authority to do so, he would build a lighthouse to mark the site and warn other mariners of the dangerous Diamond Shoals.

Later, Hamilton was indeed in such a position, having become an important leader in the Revolutionary War and later secretary of the treasury in George Washington's cabinet. Keeping his promise, he urged Congress to build a lighthouse at Cape Hatteras. In 1803, a sandstone tower rising ninety feet was completed for the small sum of $14,302. In clear weather, its light shone a distance of eighteen miles at sea, but in poor weather, if the light wasn't extinguished by storms, the small whale-oil lamp could hardly be seen beyond the shoals. And if it was, it was often confused with the lights of passing steamships and proved of almost no use to the sailors who depended on it. As Lieutenant David Porter of the United States Navy wrote, "Hatteras Light, the most important on our coast, is, without doubt, the *worst* light in the world." It took the loss of many lives and much lobbying over several years to improve the light.

One of the best-known figures of coastal Carolina folklore is Theodosia Burr Alston. Her ship vanished north of Cape Hatteras on January 2, 1813, on its way to New York, where she was to reunite with her father, the former vice president of the United States, Aaron Burr. Ironically, Burr was the man who killed Alexander Hamilton, for whom the Cape Hatteras Lighthouse was appreciatively dubbed "Hamilton's Light."

Theodosia was the only surviving child of Aaron Burr and Theodosia Bartow Prevost, a widow ten years his senior who died of cancer in 1794. Burr, an ambitious attorney, became a member of the New York assembly, then a senator, and eventually vice president. But despite each career advancement, he remained a devoted single parent to Theodosia and groomed the precocious girl as his political confidante and the mistress of his Richmond Hill country estate. According to Richard Côté, Theodosia's biographer, Aaron Burr's plans for her were far more ambitious than simply "rearing a superior woman-child." Though she spoke several languages and carried on political conversations with her father's distinguished guests at Richmond Hill, it was Burr's greatest hope that his daughter's career would surpass anything her gender had seen before. In short, he longed for the day when she would attain the highest seat in government—the one he himself had never achieved.

In 1800, at the height of his political career, Aaron Burr had received an equal number of electoral votes as Thomas Jefferson for the presidency of the United States. The decision of which man would become president and which would become vice president was left to Congress, of which Alexander Hamilton was a prominent member. Using all his resources, Hamilton apparently urged his fellows to favor Jefferson. For the next four years, Hamilton and Burr were bitter rivals and carried on a public political battle that eventually ended in a duel and Hamilton's death. Though duels were customarily engaged in as a means of settling arguments, they were nevertheless illegal, and the event ruined Burr's career. Hamilton was lauded as a national hero, while Burr was accused by Hamilton's supporters of being a traitor. Eventually, Burr was acquitted of charges of treason. But left with a career in shambles, he fled the country to Europe, where he lived for four years in self-imposed exile.

Theodosia married Joseph Alston, an ambitious lawyer and wealthy South Carolina plantation owner primed to be governor. She became the mistress of his thirteen-hundred-acre rice plantation and, in 1802, a new mother to son Aaron Burr Alston. Despite her father's reservations about her marrying when she clearly had a higher calling, Theodosia initially thrived with Joseph Alston. But as her father's career became embroiled in controversy, she found herself in a constant state of agitation. She wanted to be with him. When that wasn't possible, she and her father exchanged impassioned letters.

The difficult birth of her son and the hullabaloo surrounding her father's career left Theodosia physically and mentally exhausted. Despite pampering by servants at her South Carolina plantation home, her health continued to decline. According to Richard Côté, the birth of her son left her permanently debilitated "with a prolapsed uterus and recurring uterine infections—and possibly dying of cancer."

Still, when news came from her father that he was returning to New York, Theodosia summoned the physical strength to make the journey from Charleston to Albany to see him. It was five years since she'd last spent time with him. Despite a raging war with Britain and the threat of pirates, she prepared to make the trip with her young son.

A month later, however, tragedy struck as the ten-year-old contracted malaria and died. Theodosia's profound despair so worried her husband and father that both agreed the best thing to alleviate her suffering was to carry on with her plans to make the trip to New York.

She could have traveled by land, but her health was judged too delicate for the arduous two-week journey by carriage, so arrangements were made for her to go by sea. Joseph Alston was reluctant about a sea voyage, for he thought the trip too dangerous with the War of 1812 fully under way and the Royal Navy blockading the coast. But Theodosia refused to listen to reason. She pressed her husband to make plans for her trip and wrote letters to her father soliciting his help with the matter as well. Aaron Burr replied by sending a good friend to personally escort her. When Dr. Timothy Greene arrived, Joseph Alston was insulted that his father-in-law had so little confidence in his ability to ensure his wife's safe passage. Dr. Greene assured the younger man that Burr's only concern was the health of his daughter, and that was why he'd sent a doctor.

It's been reported that Joseph Alston wrote a letter to British naval officers in the area, begging the safe passage of his wife on her way to visit her father after the death of their only child. He was confident the officers would grant his request as a courtesy, as he was the newly appointed governor of South Carolina. By law, he was not allowed to leave the state himself during a time of war. Still, he trusted that— assuming she didn't run into a hurricane or pirates—his beloved Theodosia would arrive in New York safely.

Little did he know that those very forces lay waiting for the *Patriot*, the chartered schooner Theodosia was to take, which had previously been hired as a privateer. Its government-sponsored mission had been to raid British shipping in the West Indies. In fact, at the time of its commission to carry Theodosia to New York, its hold was said to be filled with loot. Cannons were moved below deck, and the boat was painted to disguise its recent status as a small raider.

On December 31, 1812, Joseph Alston accompanied Theodosia, her French maid, her personal cook, and Dr. Greene to the mouth of Winyah Bay in Georgetown Harbor, South Carolina. From there, the party was rowed out to the *Patriot*, where Alston bid his wife and her fellow passengers farewell. "The wind was moderate and fair," he wrote to his father-in-law. And yet the *Patriot* never reached its destination. No one ever saw the ship or any of its passengers again.

What became of the *Patriot* has been the source of speculation now for approaching two hundred years. It is commonly believed that a storm hit the North Carolina coast at the time when the ship was passing Cape Hatteras and the pale glow of Hamilton's Light. According to Richard Côté, the captain of the *Patriot* must have been holding close to shore just north of Hatteras on the night of January 2, 1813. The ship likely took a fierce beating and "probably sank between 6 P.M. Saturday and 8 A.M. Sunday," according to Côté's research.

But if you believe the tales of wizened old Banker folk, there is more to the story than that. Some believe the *Patriot* survived the storm, though just barely. It was heavily damaged and had lost its bearings when a light appeared in the distance. The captain ordered his small crew to make sail for what he thought was another ship so that he could inquire from its captain their location. Apparently, he wasn't aware of the tactics of local pirates. What he thought was the light of a nearby ship was, in fact, a trick. Pirates were known to tie a lantern to the neck of a horse and lead it up and down the beach in hopes of luring passing ships to their ruin. When the boats smashed into the rocks, they killed any survivors and made off with whatever spoils were stored in the ships' holds.

Once the pirates piled aboard the foundering *Patriot*, they murdered the captain and crew and forced everyone in

Theodosia's traveling party, including Dr. Greene, who was sworn to protect her, to walk the plank. Witnessing such violence after all she had endured—the ruin of her father's career, the death of her beloved son, the fearsome storm that had nearly done them in—Theodosia went stark raving mad. Seeing so refined a woman behave so outrageously, the pirates guffawed and cursed and made crude remarks. But they left the black-eyed, auburn-haired Theodosia alone and later took her ashore. In her arms, she clutched a portrait of herself she'd planned on giving her father as a reminder of her love and devotion.

What happened to Theodosia after that is also uncertain. Supposedly, the portrait turned up later at the home of an old woman named Polly Mann, who was paid a house call by a doctor named William Poole. Upon being treated by the doctor, the old woman admitted she had no money and regretfully could not pay him. The doctor had been admiring a portrait hanging on the wall of the old woman's crudely built cottage. The little beach-side house was constructed mostly of the "timbers from wrecks and thatched together with reeds," according to the doctor's daughter, who accompanied him. The old woman's first husband, Joseph Tillet, who had apparently been a "wrecker"—that is, he, like many poor Outer Banks residents, made his living by salvaging what could be rescued from the wrecks that washed ashore. Wreckers were known to be nearly as brutal as pirates and weren't above luring ships into the rocks themselves, or so some say.

The story Joseph Tillet told her was that he and some other men found the *Patriot* in good working condition some distance north of Cape Hatteras. When they boarded the ship, they found it completely abandoned and its cabins in disarray, though there was nothing to suggest there had been a struggle.

The old woman then proceeded to show the doctor a

trunk filled with relics from Tillet's long-ago rescue. According to Dr. Poole's daughter, the trunk held two black dresses made of homespun silk, a black lace shawl, a vase of wax flowers under a globe, and a nautilus shell. The portrait was painted on mahogany and framed in gilt. Dr. Poole accepted it as payment for his services and took it back to his home, where it remained for many years until it eventually made its way to the Lewis Walpole Library of Yale University.

Theodosia's body was never found. Countless scenarios have circulated about her surviving the wreck and living with pirates or Indians or in a catatonic state before ultimately throwing herself into the sea.

But one thing has been consistently reported since the disappearance of the *Patriot*, and that is the story of her ghost appearing on the beach near the Cape Hatteras Lighthouse. Plagued in life by one disaster after another, she is equally tormented in death, for the story goes that her wretched spirit cannot rest until she finds the portrait she was to give her father upon their meeting. More gaunt and hollow-eyed than ever, she combs the shore beneath the light of her father's old nemesis.

On stormy nights, Coast Guardsmen and fisherman alike have reported seeing the spectral figure of a woman heading north toward where the *Patriot* likely wrecked. She rummages the beach as if searching for something. Wearing an old-fashioned, long, flowing dress, she turns a haggard face to anyone who calls her. Then she mysteriously vanishes with no more trace of who she is or what she is searching for than has ever been discovered about the *Patriot*, which evaporated into thin air one January night long ago under the beam of Hamilton's Light.

In 1854, Hamilton's Light was made taller and refitted with a first-order Fresnel lens, a vast improvement over the original design. But shelling during the Civil War left it too damaged to repair. And since the expensive Fresnel lens had been stolen by retreating Confederates, the Lighthouse Board decided to tear down the old structure and start anew.

The present Cape Hatteras Light is the tallest lighthouse in the nation, measuring 198 feet to the focal plane of its lens. It flashes every seven seconds and is visible for twenty-four nautical miles out to sea. Completed and first lit in 1870, the gigantic lighthouse was given one final touch a few years later—its distinctive black and white barbershop striping.

Congress spared no expense in constructing what would become the nation's most recognizable—and some say most majestic—lighthouse. Built before the advent of the pile driver, the new Cape Hatteras Light was erected upon a foundation that "floated" on two layers of pine timbers laid crossways in an airtight pit below sea level. Though the beach eroded so severely over the succeeding century that the ocean threatened to topple the massive tower, the submerged timbers were found to be perfectly intact in 1999 when the lighthouse underwent a monumental relocation. Despite attempts to slow erosion by constructing barrier walls and laying sandbags, the lighthouse teetered on the edge of the Atlantic, just 120 feet from the water, by 1987. When it was built in 1870, the beacon had stood 1,600 feet from shore.

In 1999, the International Chimney Corporation of Buffalo, New York, safely moved the tower 2,900 feet, placing it in the exact same proximity to the ocean as it had been originally. The move cost $12 million and was named the most outstanding civil-engineering achievement of 2000 by the American Society of Civil Engineers.

"Besides being an incredible engineering feat, this project spoke volumes about the American spirit," said Francis Peltier, superintendent of Cape Hatteras National Seashore.

"Our generation stepped up to the challenge in the same manner that the lighthouse keepers stepped up to the challenge of making the nation's coastline safe for people who made their living by the sea. We have, by our actions, passed on to future generations a vessel of the American experience, an icon of what's best about the American character, a tangible object that our grandchildren and their children can visit and touch. We have provided a window through which they can view the greatness of our national past and come to know who we are as a people and a nation."

To reach the Cape Hatteras Lighthouse by land, follow US 64 from the mainland across Roanoke Island to the Outer Banks. At Whalebone Junction, turn south onto NC 12, which leads about fifty miles down the Outer Banks to Buxton and the lighthouse. Or, for a trip you'll long remember, you can take a toll ferry ride of over two and a half hours from either Swan Quarter off US 264 or Cedar Island off US 70/NC 12. Either ferry will take you and your car to Ocracoke Island. You can then drive to the northeast tip of Ocracoke to catch a free ferry to the southern end of Hatteras Island. You can check ferry schedules by visiting www.outer-banks.com/ferry. From the southern end of Hatteras Island, drive north on NC 12 toward Buxton. You'll see the lighthouse before you reach the signs for the entrance. For more information, call the Cape Hatteras National Seashore headquarters in Manteo at 252-473-2111 or the Buxton Visitor Center at 252-995-4474.

On April 18, 2003, the lighthouse was reopened to the public after its move. Tickets go on sale each morning at eight o'clock in the booth outside the gift shop. They are available on a first-come, first-served basis. Get yours early, if possible, as only a limited number are sold each day, and they sometimes sell out before noon. If you miss your chance at climbing the 268 stairs to the top, don't fret. The grounds are open year-round, so you can still take pictures and visit the keeper's quarters and gift shops. And don't forget to walk down to the original site of the lighthouse, where you'll find the engraved stones of both the 1803 and 1870 towers, which bear the names of the courageous keepers who once manned the stations.

North Island Light, Georgetown
© *2004 Bob and Sandra Shanklin, the "Lighthouse People"*

THE YOUNG GUARDIAN

GEORGETOWN LIGHT (NORTH ISLAND LIGHT)
NEAR GEORGETOWN, SOUTH CAROLINA

"He is safe from danger who is on his guard even
when safe."

Publilius Syrus, *Maxims*

Ten miles downstream from the historic inland port of
Georgetown lies North Island. At its southernmost tip stands
the eighty-seven-foot-tall North Island Lighthouse, the third
sentinel built on the site to mark the mouth of Winyah
Bay. In colonial times, Georgetown was a bustling seaport
where Low Country goods such as indigo and rice were
loaded onto ships bound for Europe. At one time, half of
the rice in this country came from Georgetown. By the
mid-1800s, more rice sailed out of Georgetown Harbor than
any other port in the world. "Carolina Gold" was an international favorite.

But entering and traversing the narrow channel of
Winyah Bay was dangerous. Bordered by salt marshes and
plagued with shifting sand bars and oyster beds, the bay itself

is treacherous to maneuver, but add to that the dangerous granite jetty that extends from South Island to the shipping channel at North Island and you can quickly understand why a lighthouse was needed to guide ships into the harbor. In 1789, Paul Trapier, a Revolutionary War hero, donated a strip of land upon which he hoped a lighthouse would be built. The newly created Lighthouse Service, however, did not act upon Trapier's bequest until 1799, a full decade later.

Once construction was under way, the lighthouse was completed in just under two years. Built of ancient cypress wood, it stood seventy-two feet tall. Though it was said to be a sturdy structure, the lighthouse gave way during a raging storm in 1806. Following that, Congress set aside money for a brick or stone lighthouse on the same site. By 1812, the second light was operational. Like its predecessor, it was seventy-two feet tall. Made of brick, painted white, and capped with a black lantern room, it served as a daytime landmark for mariners crossing the bay.

The lighthouse that stands at North Island today was built in 1867 to replace the 1812 tower, which was severely damaged during the Civil War. Built of rubble stone, it stands eighty-seven feet tall and has walls six feet thick at the base. Unlike most lighthouses, the North Island Light has a solid cut-stone staircase instead of the more common spiral stairs of cast-iron construction.

A string of light keepers lived and worked at the station over the years, but none left behind a more poignant story than one who manned the light in the early 1800s. With only his young daughter, Annie, by his side, the keeper accepted the challenge of maintaining the lighthouse, a role usually shared by an assistant or one's spouse. Thought to be seven or eight years old and small for her age, Annie was incapable of doing much work around the station and also required a great deal of attention herself. Having no wife to look after the child, the keeper took the girl with him wherever he went. He learned to allow twice as much time for every task, as he was required to perform the dual roles of being the primary caregiver to his young daughter and light keeper of the station throughout the long day. Only at night did he dare part from the girl. As she lay sleeping, he watched the light and wound the clockworks. When time allowed, he worked ahead of schedule, carrying twice as much whale oil up the tower as necessary and cleaning the lantern-room windows to save from doing it the next day. It was difficult work under the best of conditions, and even more so for Annie's father. But by making such adjustments, the keeper managed the station well and still looked after his little daughter as best he could.

One day, the keeper and Annie climbed into their small wooden boat and set a course for Georgetown to replenish their supplies. Every other week or so, the pair made the trip, crossing Winyah Bay at a time when the current would help carry the rowboat into the harbor and then returning as the tide washed back out to sea, which saved the keeper from expending energy rowing against waves that outmatched him.

Rising before dawn, the twosome pushed off from the island and rode serenely over the gently rolling waves, making landfall at Georgetown just as the sun crossed the bay and lit the windows of the Kaminski House and the old market building near the Sampit River. Annie, cozied up with her doll in the hull of the boat, dozed awhile longer as her father rowed the boat quietly through the channel. On the air was the perfume of Georgetown—the smell of chimney smoke rising from the shops and dwellings lining the harbor, commingled with the briny smack the flood tide carried with it from the mouth of the bay.

Rousing Annie, the keeper docked the boat at the pier. Together, he and his drowsy daughter went in search of provisions. Before long, Annie was wide awake, chatting with the shopkeepers and marking off items from the list her father had given her. "What's next?" he asked.

She scanned the list for the answer. "Thread."

"Oh, yes," her father said. "For Dolly's poor arm. How's she managing?"

Annie whispered in her doll's ear, then said, "Not very well."

"Oh. Perhaps we should hurry home and look after her injuries."

Annie whispered to the doll again, then held Dolly to her ear as if listening for her reply. "She says it isn't that urgent, Father. We have time for sweetmeats and comfits."

"Thank goodness," her father said. Together, the three of them—Dolly, the keeper, and Annie—made their way to the teahouse and then on to the shops, spending the entire morning looking in windows and relishing their time on the mainland.

As noon approached, a stiff wind caught the keeper's attention. "Come along, Annie," he said, warily pressing the girl to hurry back to the boat. "Dolly needn't wait any longer for us to get her on the mend. Let's get ourselves home now so we can patch her back to health before supper."

The water was still calm as they reached the pier and packed their supplies into the boat. But when the sun disappeared, the keeper quickly lifted Annie down onto the bench next to him and pushed off from the dock with one oar. Without waiting for the ebb tide to help propel them out of the harbor and down through the bay, he began rowing mightily. Annie shivered as the wind blew her curly blond locks over her eyes. She dragged a finger in the water as the boat sliced through the channel.

But immediately it began to rain, and quite fiercely. The wind blew hard against the keeper's back and rocked the boat and kicked up the water and frightened little Annie to tears. She was wet and cold and frightened. Water filled the bottom of the boat. The more it took on, the more difficult it became for the keeper to row. He let go of the oars for a moment, trying to comfort Annie, then lost control altogether as the wind slapped the oars back and forth. Waves jumped over the sides, and the keeper saw then that there was no saving the boat nor any of their supplies. Quickly, he took a length of rope floating around loose inside the boat and tied Annie to his back. With Dolly held firmly in one hand, Annie gripped her father's neck tightly as he floundered out of the boat and began swimming for their very lives.

Not knowing in which direction he swam, the keeper fought with all his might to stay afloat. The rain pounding into the surf and into his face blinded him. He didn't know how long he could persist. But there was Annie, his sweet girl, to think of, and that inspired him to perform the inhuman feat of somehow reaching the shore. He crawled to safety with Annie still fastened to his back. He collapsed, then slept through the rest of the evening, awakening just as dawn washed the sky in blue and orange.

Oh, he was never so grateful to be alive, and to have Annie with him! He called to her, but the girl slumbered on. "Annie," he called again, then shook his body to wake the sleepyhead lying on his back. Again, she did not stir. And when the keeper at last untied himself from his daughter, he discovered his sweet child had drowned during their dreadful struggle.

Afterward, the keeper became despondent, leaving his chores at the light station undone. Wandering into Georgetown in bewilderment, he searched the teahouse for his little daughter, calling out her name and falling to his knees in grief when she did not answer.

But if you believe the tales of fishermen, Annie is still around. Since the girl's death, mariners have claimed she comes aboard their vessels, warning them of impending hurricanes and nor'easters. Often, the weather is mild and sunny, just as it was the day of her death. When they receive a visit from Annie, wise sailors draw up their traps and nets and set a course home. Those who don't, it is said, are sure to perish.

Listed on the National Register of Historic Places, North Island Light still serves as an active aid to mariners. The property is privately owned, however, and though the tower is not open for touring, the owners allow visitors to come up to the high-tide mark on the beach, close enough to take good photos. The island can be reached only by boat. Private tours are offered from Georgetown. For information, call Rover Tours at 800-705-9063 or 843-546-8822 or visit www.rovertours.com.

THE BLOODSTAINED FLOOR

CAPE ROMAIN LIGHT
NEAR MCCLELLANVILLE, SOUTH CAROLINA

"Blood, though it sleep a time, yet never dies.
The gods on murtherers fix revengeful eyes."

George Chapman, *The Widow's Tears*

Two towers stand on Lighthouse Island. One is tall, brick, octagonal, and painted black and white. The other is squattier and painted red. It's an unusual sight, two lights standing at the same location, as it was customary to tear down the older structure when it was replaced by a more advanced beacon. It did happen on occasion, however, that older lights were left standing alongside their proxies, not only at Cape Romain but also at places like Cape Henry, Virginia, and Point Loma, California.

Perhaps the most uncharacteristic thing about the station at Lighthouse Island is that it was the setting for a violent murder, confessed to by a former keeper as he lay dying years later. The story goes that a Norwegian keeper named Fischer and his wife settled at the light station in the mid-1800s. It was an isolated and inhospitable location, visited only rarely by outsiders brave enough to chance the shifting sand bars surrounding the island. At that time, the nearest town was Charleston, though it was still a good distance away. Even the tender was an infrequent caller, arriving with supplies sometimes only once or twice a year, an inconvenience that vexed the keeper's wife, whose insistence on fresh-baked bread with each meal left her continually longing for stores of flour and baking powder.

But in the beginning, the Fischers looked upon their stay at Cape Romain with optimism. The keeper looked after the light, and his wife kept the house neat as a new pin and cooked large Scandinavian meals. When salmon was available, she prepared *gravlax*. But more often, they ate a bountiful assortment of raw fish and shrimp. Whenever possible, she sent the keeper out for venison and wild game so she could make *spekemat*. White-tailed deer was not nearly as tasty as reindeer or moose, but covered in creamy sauce, it sufficed.

To pass time, Mrs. Fischer busied herself with embroidery. She enjoyed all kinds of thread work—pattern darning, cross-stitching, hardanger embroidery. She even undertook a batch of "white work" on the neckbands and wristbands of her husband's linen shirts. Indeed, there was plenty to occupy her for a good long time.

But after a while, the keeper's wife began to complain. "I miss my family," she told her husband. "I should like very much to make a short visit home to Norway."

"Soon," he promised, provoking Mrs. Fischer's indignation. She detested nothing more than insincerity and found her husband's pledge a glib one meant to quiet her.

"You don't mean it," she said. "But I do. I mean to travel home to Hammerfest, and I will."

"But why?" the keeper wanted to know. "We have our own lives to lead."

Cape Romain Light
© *2004 Bob and Sandra Shanklin, the "Lighthouse People"*

"Just to see my mother's face. A woman misses her mother and father, all her family. I miss them all so terribly much. My stay needn't be long, just a few weeks."

"A few weeks!"

"Five at the most."

"Five!" her husband said. "And who am *I* to talk to for so long an absence?"

Mrs. Fischer doubted her husband would miss her presence much at all, but it was not her nature to quarrel. A good Norwegian wife held her tongue. Mrs. Fischer prided herself on being a dutiful companion—not just once, but twice, for she had been married previously and had remained a devoted and dutiful wife until her first husband's death. She had thought of him from time to time since arriving on the island and lately had begun to miss him as well as her family far away in the old country. Of course, she never mentioned it to the keeper, whose good humor had waned with the seasons and the worsening weather.

Her first husband had left her a small fortune in gold coins and fine jewelry, and now she fancied spending a little of it for a return to Norway. She was beginning to loathe the monotony of work without respite. A trip would do her good, return the sense of wonder she'd felt for the island in the beginning, make her appreciate its wild beauty again.

But now she longed for the spectacular fjords and mountains of her beloved Hammerfest. She missed the midnight sun of late spring and summer and the marvelous northern lights of winter.

The keeper, however, feared his wife would never return if she left, so he locked her valuables in a small trunk and placed it on the mantel, where he could keep a watchful eye on it. He meant to keep an eye on her as well.

"Those are mine," she protested. "You've no right to keep them from me."

Incensed, he suddenly turned on her. "I am your

husband," he said, stepping closer, backing her to the wall. Darkness shrouded his features in the dimly lit parlor, but she saw the corners of his lips curl slightly. "I have every right." She felt his gaze upon her, and it cooled her blood. She could hardly believe he was capable of being annoyed with her, let alone that he should lash out so spitefully. Startled, she let the issue die.

But as time passed, she found life on the island utterly miserable, especially now that her husband had driven a wedge between them. She began stealing glances at the locked trunk on the mantel. If only she could get her hands on it when he wasn't looking.

One blustery night when the keeper was tending the light, Mrs. Fischer tied on a head scarf and donned a heavy woolen cape. Then she took the trunk from the mantel and sneaked away from the keeper's house in search of the small boat they used to ferry out to meet the tender. She knew that the sand bars were treacherous and that Charleston was farther away than the dinghy could safely carry her. Most likely, she would die at sea. But staying on the island with a man she no longer trusted, no longer knew, was out of the question.

She was nearly to the boat when someone called her name. "Marta!" she heard through the trees. It was her husband. "Mar-ta O-les-dat-ter!" She tried to quicken her pace, but the cumbersome strongbox slowed her progress. Inside it was everything of value she owned in the world—silver brooches that once fastened her skirts and sashes, both of her gold wedding crowns edged with small silver bangles, meant to tinkle and ward off evil spirits. She couldn't conceive how she would fare on her own without something with which to barter. Even so, she quickly buried the trunk in the sand and made haste to reach the dock before her husband could catch her. She recognized the irritation in his voice, despite his attempts to hide it. He meant to punish her—that she knew.

Then, suddenly, he was behind her, grabbing at the damask scarf on her head, pulling it loose, and snatching for her thick braids. Mrs. Fischer screamed, but struggling was useless. The keeper was a large man, and he yanked with such force that it loosened the pins holding the braids in two neat coils at either side of her head. He grabbed again and caught one of the braids, which had flopped free in the skirmish. When he jerked, tears welled in her eyes. Still, she fought with all the mettle of her Viking ancestors, kicking and lashing out in defense. In the end, however, he dragged her back to the keeper's house, where he took a long knife from the cupboard and, after much taunting, cut off her beautiful braids and tossed them in her face.

By then, Mrs. Fischer knew her murder was imminent. She warned him that if he spilled a drop of her blood, she would call his name from the grave. And according to witnesses living at Cape Romain after the murder, she kept her promise.

When the evil deed was done, the keeper buried his wife on the island. He told those who inquired some months later that the poor woman had gone mad and taken her own life. No one ever doubted him. But on his deathbed, the Norwegian confessed to the killing, having been tormented by the eerie bloodstain left for him as a reminder of what he'd done.

No amount of scrubbing was ever able to rid the floor of its mark, not even later when August Wichmann became the light keeper. Wichmann's wife scoured the spot repeatedly, only to have the stain return again and again. According to the Wichmanns' son, Fred, other strange things happened at the lighthouse as well. On windless nights, the keeper often heard footsteps on the wooden stairs of the tower. Thinking it one of his assistants, he would open the trapdoor leading from the lantern room down the stairs, only to find no one there. In time, he came to believe the sounds belonged to the restless spirit of Mrs. Fischer, who longed to have her death avenged.

Today, the two towers stand alone. The keeper's house is gone. And though subsequent light keepers and their families tended Mrs. Fischer's grave for many years, the plot has been lost in a thick tangle of vegetation. As for the buried treasure, it has never been found.

Lighthouse Island is part of Cape Romain National Wildlife Refuge, located six miles offshore from McClellanville. It is accessible only by boat. McClellanville is approximately thirty-five miles north of Charleston on US 17. Private tours of the island are available through Cape Romain Marina (843-887-3330) and the Sewee Visitor and Environmental Education Center (843-928-3368).

Old Hilton Head Rear Range Light (the Leamington Light)
© 2004 Bob and Sandra Shanklin, the "Lighthouse People"

THE BLUE LADY

OF LEAMINGTON

OLD HILTON HEAD REAR RANGE LIGHT

(LEAMINGTON LIGHT)

HILTON HEAD, SOUTH CAROLINA

"He first deceased; she for a little tried
To live without him, liked it not, and died."

Sir Henry Wotton, "Upon the Death of Sir Albertus
Morton's Wife"

Today, Hilton Head Island is a resort comprised mainly of ten well-heeled gated communities marketed by developers as "residential plantations." These "plantations" follow roughly the boundaries of their authentic antebellum forebears, large slaveholding estates that once grew indigo and rice and the king of Southern crops, cotton. It was cotton that made South Carolina one of the wealthiest states in the Union. And Hilton Head was the first island to grow the moneymaking bolls, beginning in 1790. Soon, sea-island cotton was considered the finest in the world.

One of Hilton Head's most prominent plantations was Leamington, located on the eastern portion of the island and bordered by the Atlantic Ocean on one side and Broad Creek on the other. When Union forces stormed the island in November 1861 shortly after Confederates fired on Fort Sumter in Charleston Harbor, it was Leamington Plantation where they established their camp, where they transferred prisoners of war and the wounded, and where they eventually built the island's first lighthouse.

When the war ended, the Federals returned to the North and the old way of life resumed, for the most part. Homes that had been pillaged and burned were rebuilt. Crops were replanted. And cotton returned with a vengeance.

For a brief time, Hilton Head landowners prospered again until the appearance of a tiny gray beetle called the boll weevil. Feeding on cotton bolls faster than planters could contend with it, the boll weevil became a blight that decimated crops and eventually wiped out cotton on the island altogether.

Following that, Hilton Head was soon forgotten by the world. Wealthy plantation families were either bankrupted by the blight or else moved away, leaving the island to a handful of white planters and freed slaves, who settled on the lands of their former owners.

By the time lighthouse keeper Adam Fripp and his twenty-one-year-old daughter, Caroline, came to Hilton Head to man the light station, nearly three decades had passed since the Civil War. The original lighthouse erected by Union soldiers had been destroyed in a storm, and a set of range lights now replaced it. One light shone from the top of the keeper's house itself, and the other stood over a mile away on a tall, skeletal tower that rose ninety-five feet into the air. When mariners navigating the waters around the island saw the flashing light of the keeper's house, they then looked for the fixed white light of the taller tower behind it. When the two lights were aligned so that one sat atop the other, sailors knew the water was deep and safe.

Little is known about Adam and Caroline Fripp except that the two had lived alone since Caroline's mother's death. The surname Fripp, however, is rooted deeply in Hilton Head history, and it's likely that Adam and Caroline were the descendants of one of the several Fripp families who'd been plantation owners on the island. All that's known for sure is that Caroline was fiercely attached to her father and that he was equally enamored of her.

According to legend, Caroline enjoyed life on the island a great deal. But she was also curious to hear tales of life abroad, often greeting sailors stopping over on their journeys with a flurry of questions. "Tell me quick, Henry, where've you been?" she once asked her favorite sailor with unabashed familiarity.

"London," he said.

"Oh, London! Father, London, did you hear?" And without waiting for a reply, she added, "Lilian Bell says Englishwomen are much more assertive than American women."

"Not counting you, I presume," Henry said, teasing.

"Oh, go on," Caroline told him, flattered that she might actually be seen as the "new woman" Lilian Bell wrote of in her articles. "If I live long enough, I *will* visit Regent Street, Henry, and I'll go to all the finest boutiques there—Jay's, and Lewis's, and Allenby's, for sure."

"And what would you buy there, pretty Caroline?"

"Oh, Henry, what wouldn't I buy, if I could? First, I'd

buy a gauze theater bonnet. And a card case. Then again, Lilian says Dresden is the best place to buy leather goods. And I'd find a dress, an exquisite blue taffeta dress with a gored skirt. But that would have to be from Paris. Lilian Bell says shopping in Paris is one of the greatest pleasures to be found 'in this vale of tears.' Her words exactly."

"A theater bonnet? On Hilton Head?" her father asked. "Lilian Bell, huh?"

"Yes, Father. Lilian Bell. Lilian says Paris is really much more convenient than our larger department stores here in America."

"Where in America, exactly?"

"Oh, you know, Father. New York, of course. Lilian says there are only four cities in the world where a girl should buy clothes—New York, London, Paris, and Vienna. Oh, but no, not Paris. I mean, most decidedly, I would buy a blue dress in Vienna. Lilian says Viennese fashions are just as elegant as Parisian styles but more modest in nature. 'Paris clothes generally look immoral when you buy them,' she says, 'and feel immoral when you get them on.' Isn't that some saying, Henry?" Smiling unreservedly, Caroline then just as quickly painted a frown on her face and slid her arm in the crook of Henry's elbow. "Dear Henry, you must understand better than Father that a girl needs a woman's guidance in such matters."

And wishing for nothing more in his life than to turn and ask Caroline to marry him and sail off together to see all the big world she longed for—just as countless other sailors must have wished, he reckoned—Henry simply smiled and let her go on and on. For he knew that no matter how much she spoke of traveling, Caroline would never leave her father.

Still, seeing her standing so straight with her sun-streaked hair twisted up neatly in a bun at the back of her head, seeing her lovely flat back and small waist, he could envision her in the blue dress of which she spoke. And he meant to find that dress if he could, meant to see her face when she came running up to him all a-sparkle with questions about where he'd been, meant to hear her laughter pealing across the wind-swept island and drowning out the ocean.

"Henry? Are you listening?"

Then, pulling back from somewhere deep within himself, Henry covered his misstep. "I nearly bought a Persian carpet awhile back in Constantinople."

Caroline looked worried. "But Henry, Lilian says there is nothing so unsatisfactory as postponing a purchase. For in nine cases out of ten, she says, you'll never see the same article again."

"Indeed, I haven't," Henry said, resuming their walk. "But I've no place for a rug anyway."

"Honestly, Henry. It's just as well. Lilian says the bazaars of the Orient are dens of thieves and that you have to be trickier than a Chinese diplomat to deal with them."

At this, Henry laughed full-bellied, not stopping until the three of them arrived at the door to the keeper's house. Once inside, Caroline's father soon edged out his daughter for Henry's attention. They drank cups of cider and exchanged news of the weather.

But never was she truly out of either man's thoughts. And after Henry sailed, the light keeper resumed doting unrivaled over his daughter, half worried in his secret heart that he was keeping her from the life she wanted and deserved with her young suitor. Still, the light keeper was not a young man anymore, and he needed his daughter to help him at his labor. It was important work, his, and kept sailors like Henry safe to visit the island another day. There was still time for them yet, Adam Fripp reasoned, still plenty of time.

And though Caroline felt strongly for Henry, she gladly walked a mile alongside her father every day to the rear range light, chatting not only about Lilian Bell but all sorts of other things Adam Fripp cared little about. He simply enjoyed her company as they walked through the tangle of sea oats to the faded gray lighthouse. Once there, he handed Caroline linen rags and ammonia and sent her ahead up the tower to polish the windows for the night watch. Then, carrying hefty cans of oil, he followed her, nudging her along each time she stopped and turned with what she thought some fascinating point but that Adam considered prattle. He loved his daughter, but—heaven help her—she could bend one's ear like no one he'd ever seen. "Yes," he would say on occasion, as attentively as possible. Or "I see." But really, he seldom heard anything Caroline said. She was more company than any man needed. And he might have been the wind for all the company he gave her.

He felt he'd done poorly by Caroline. She was such a gregarious girl and had a deep yearning for companionship. And what an imagination! She'd never been to the theater or a department store in all her born years. But to hear her talk, one got the impression she was a world-class holidaymaker.

"Father, I met a most interesting fellow at the hunt club," she said as they reached the landing of the lantern room.

"The what, my dear?"

"The hunt club, Father. Nearby. Oh, Father, you simply must go out with me more often."

"Do you mean people are actually paying money to hunt and fish here?"

"Naturally, Father. The man I met says that someday this whole place will be a resort."

"A what?"

"A resort, Father. Paradise. People will come from all over the world to hunt and fish and do all sorts of things here."

Her father scoffed. "Let them endure one nor'easter and see how fond they are of paradise then."

And nothing more prophetic was spoken by Adam Fripp than those very words, for that August a destructive hurricane struck the island while he and Caroline were separated.

Caroline had just recently received from Henry the most beautiful blue taffeta dress she'd ever imagined. "Oh, Henry!" she'd said. "You're so generous to me. You're simply the dearest man in the world. After Father, of course," she added, smiling charmingly and then holding the garment to her waist and whirling around.

"Well, go and try it on, for land's sake," her father had said. "A man wants to see if his money's well spent. Right, Henry?"

Henry stammered, not sure what to say precisely.

"He's only tormenting you," Caroline said. "You needn't be bothered."

"Oh, it's not . . . I mean, I don't mind that . . . ," Henry said.

Caroline laughed. "Oh, all right then." And into the house she disappeared, returning shortly all primped and coiffed for the men's opinions. Neither spoke, however, for between them, they'd never seen anything as striking as she was in the fashionable garment, which seemed tailored for her and no one else. And surely, it was made just so, for Henry had memorized her measurements—not from having been told them but from knowing that, standing before him, her head came exactly level with his lower lip, when it was parted, just barely, from the other. And that her shoulders were four inches narrower on either side than his jacket, which she'd often worn on their walks from the docks to the house. And that her waist was the size of a daisy chain just fourteen links long that he'd made as a necklace for her. He dallied away much of that day with Caroline and Adam, hoping to summon the courage to ask for her hand in marriage. But Caroline was simply too excited to sit still. Eventually, Henry had to set a course away from the island. A storm was coming, and he needed to be far out at sea to miss it.

Afterward, Caroline had scarcely been able to keep from staring at herself in the looking glass. "Can you believe it, Father?" she said. "What on earth gave him such a notion? Oh, I don't care," she added before Adam could answer, a slight look of worry crossing her face. "I'll never leave you, Father. You mustn't fear that. Henry and I will . . . Well, silly me." And she was up again, reaching out to her reflection in the mirror, marveling over the dress's every silken pleat.

Later, when it was time to walk to the rear range light, Caroline's silence betrayed her effort to dutifully assist her father as usual. She wouldn't dream of rushing him, for she knew he was not as young as he used to be.

But Adam Fripp could tell that she wanted not to go, not this day—that what she wanted more than anything was to return home, stand before the looking glass, and admire the new blue dress. "My dear," he said, turning to face her, "you've much to think about. Go on home. I can manage."

"Absolutely not, Father. There's a storm coming. Why, I wouldn't dream of it."

"Wouldn't you?" he said, smiling kindly.

"Well, I . . . No! Of course not."

But Adam Fripp for once outspoke his daughter. "Now, Caroline, there is nothing so useless as a new dress hanging on a nail. I believe Lilian Bell said something along those lines, did she not? Or else she should have. And I agree with the good woman. I want you to go home and enjoy yourself, Caroline. Put on your dress, and when I return, we'll dance. And once this little storm is over, we'll make a trip to Beaufort, maybe even Savannah. You'd like that, wouldn't you?"

"Oh, Father, yes, of course, but—"

"And we'll go to the theater, if they have one there."

Caroline laughed. "In Savannah, you mean?"

"And we'll see, ah . . . What would Miss Lilian Bell recommend, do you think?"

Caroline started to answer.

"You ponder it while you're getting ready, my darling. And pick me out something fitting to wear, if you don't mind. I know I haven't the wardrobe of a true gentleman, but I'm sure you'll find something suitable."

"Of course I will," Caroline said, smiling with all her soul.

"All right, then. Off you go."

And with that, Caroline hugged her father's neck and went home.

The storm walloped the island, and Adam Fripp did not return to dance with his daughter as promised. After much wringing of hands, Caroline ran out into the tempest to find him. Still wearing the blue taffeta dress Henry had given her, she plunged through sand and surf, through sea oats lashing her like a million small whips, until she reached the tower. She was halfway up the stairs when a great gust of wind sent debris flying into the lantern room, shattering the glass. A half-second later, the lamp was blown out. Just at that moment, she heard her father cry out from where he'd fallen on the stairs, clutching his chest. She ran to him.

"Caroline, you must get the light burning."

"Let me help you to the lantern room."

"There isn't time. You must hurry, Caroline. The storm is terribly strong, and men depend on your doing it. Do you understand?"

"Yes, Father, but you're frightening me."

Adam Fripp spoke with great pain. "I love you, my dear."

"I love you, too, Father," Caroline said, wrapping her arms around him and weeping. "I'm so frightened. What do I do?"

But when she loosened her embrace, she found her father was dead—and with him all her own reasons for living. She felt as if she could not go on without him—or didn't want to, at least. All was dark without him.

Then she remembered that the light had been extinguished. Immediately, she rose to fetch more oil. *Quickly*, she told herself.

Leaving her father on the stairs, she hurried down to the oil house and worked hastily to fill a metal canister. Afterward, she was slowed by the great labor it took to haul the can up each step. She persisted, however, for it was her father's dying wish that she should burn the light for the sailors who depended on it. Momentarily, she thought of Henry battling the storm somewhere out at sea. But before her thoughts could linger, water began seeping through the cracks around the door at the base of the tower. The rain continued without ceasing. Slowly, the water inched its way up the stairs until it threatened to engulf her father's lifeless body.

Hurrying to where he lay on the stairs, Caroline was beside herself with concern. She waited for a while to see if the water would recede. It didn't. Minute by minute, it rose higher, until finally it lapped at the sullied hem of her new dress. Poor Henry must have searched the world for that dress. She couldn't just die, as she wished now that her father was gone. She had to burn the light for Henry and all the others.

But she would not climb the stairs to the lantern room alone. Never again would she and her father be parted. Standing behind his body on the stairs, she leaned down and looped her arms under his and locked her hands in front of his chest. Then, with even more gusto than she'd summoned before with the oil can, Caroline wrestled her father's dead weight, ever so gradually making him come to rest one step higher, then another. Her slow progress kept her just barely ahead of the rising floodwaters. But she persisted all through the night. And legend says she manned the light alone for three days after the waters receded, keeping her word to her father until she could no longer persist. It was incredibly lonely without him, and despite her efforts to keep working, to keep her mind off her isolation, Caroline finally gave up. She was found dead in the lantern room beside her father a few days later, apparently overcome by grief and exhaustion.

For years, rumors circulated that on dark, stormy nights, a woman wearing a blue dress could be seen scurrying along the path between the keeper's house and the rear range light. Even after the keeper's house was moved across the island to Sea Pines in Harbour Town, people swore they'd seen the phantom of a young woman. Seeming to glow from some strange, beautiful blue iridescence, she stood in the window of the rear range lighthouse or else walked between the oil house and the base of the tower before disappearing inside.

Old Hilton Headers say it is the ghost of Caroline Fripp, the Blue Lady of Leamington, stricken with guilt for letting her father tend the light alone. She is perpetually sad faced, they say, always wearing the bedraggled blue dress from the night of the hurricane. And though she seems to be ever searching for her beloved father, the once-talkative young woman remains silent as the grave.

※

In 1967, developers bought and moved the keeper's house to Harbour Town Marina. Though another lighthouse stands in Harbour Town, it is not the Leamington Light. The lighthouse that Caroline and Adam Fripp tended now stands nearly forgotten in the middle of a golf course at Palmetto Dunes Resort. It is difficult to see from the highway through the thick canopy of pines that surrounds it, and it's virtually impossible to gain access to the light unless you're one of the privileged residents of Palmetto Dunes or the guest of a member of the Arthur Hills Golf Course. But many consider its isolation a part of the light's mystique.

To reach the Old Hilton Head Rear Range Light, take Exit 21 off I-95 and follow US 278 toward Hilton Head Island. You'll find Palmetto Dunes Resort near mile marker 8. Palmetto Dunes is a private resort. Access to the lighthouse is reserved for residents and invited guests only. Sometimes, special arrangements may be made with the developers, however. For information about scheduling a visit and obtaining a pass, contact the Greenwood Development Corporation by calling 864-941-4044 or visiting www.greenwooddevelopment.com.

A Grievous Passion

St. Simons Island Light
Near Brunswick, Georgia

"Murder is born of love, and love attains the
greatest intensity in murder."

Octave Mirbeau, *The Torture Garden*

From the moment you cross the causeway leading to St. Simons Island, you sense there's something different about the place, something secretive. Something beguiling but also a little unsettling, a little decadent. As the sun sinks into the marshes, you drift along the sandy coastal highway as it sets a course through a jumble of palmettos and live oaks tangled one tree to the next by hoary tufts of Spanish moss. The houses along the way are pastel colored and made of tabby, harking back to slave days, when people of dark skin worked the plantations set deeper into the island. The air is sultry, heavy, and tinged with Georgia honeysuckle, the wind expectant, as if rain is never more than a few seconds away. Just ahead lies the Atlantic Ocean. Tucked behind a quaint restaurant sporting red-checked tablecloths and selling galvanized buckets of crab legs is a lighthouse that in the wash of vermillion skies gleams like a jewel.

There is magic here, for sure, brought over from Africa, where conjurers called root doctors learned to fly, to make pots boil without fire, to make hoes turn over earth without hands and backs to swing them. The first lighthouse at St. Simons was built during the time when men were tricked away from their homeland of monkeys and parrots, peanuts and bananas and crops that never needed tending. Not far away from the light station is a place called Ebo Landing, where an entire tribe of Africans drowned themselves in Dunbar Creek when they tried to march back to that distant place, away from the brutal treatment of slaveholders.

Even when Confederates dynamited the lighthouse in 1862 to keep it from guiding the Union sailors who were closing in on them, and then when another tower was built ten years later to replace it, that magic lingered in the air, in the hearts of freed slaves who went about beating their drums over their dead and dancing the Buzzard Lope.

To Fred Osborne, who was assigned in 1872 to keep the light, the island seemed as wild as Africa. The standing black swamp water in the area was infested with malaria-carrying mosquitoes that had wiped out much of the population of the island and killed most of the crew building the lighthouse, including the architect, Charles Cluskey. Osborne, said to be fanatical in carrying out his duties at the station, was greatly concerned about the prospect of contracting malaria himself. In 1874, he complained to the Lighthouse Establishment about poor health conditions on the island, noting the number of stagnant ponds. Two years later, most likely after another grievance filed by the keeper, the Lighthouse Establishment completely revamped the station, weatherproofing the keepers' quarters and installing a speaking tube that carried conversations between persons

St. Simons Island Light
© *2004 Bob and Sandra Shanklin, the "Lighthouse People"*

working in the top of the lighthouse and those down below in the keeper's residence.

It was shortly after that when keeper Osborne sought to hire an assistant. According to legend, the task proved more difficult than he hoped. But those who knew the keeper said it was obvious what the trouble was—the keeper was persnickety, pure and simple.

By that time, the island had been transformed from a plantation-based community of slaves and slave owners to a thriving coastal mill town. The Georgia Land and Lumber Company had bought up most of the old rice and cotton fields and established a number of sawmills near the Frederica River. Soon, the Frederica and other local waterways carried wood products from the island to ports all over the world. Schools, churches, and all manner of other establishments sprang up on the island until no longer did it feel so isolated.

Osborne was forced to keep constant watch for ships coming and going. Because he took his work extremely seriously, he agonized over whether or not he could guide every one of the vessels into and out of the harbor safely. And in good conscience, he knew he couldn't. He desperately needed another set of eyes to scan the horizon, another strong back to haul up the fuel to the lantern room, another green thumb to help him and his wife tend the garden, and, most of all, another set of hands to polish the windows and the prisms of the lens. This was of the utmost importance, the keeper felt, though people on the island thought his exactness at cleaning the glass a little peculiar. It was no wonder he needed help—his fastidiousness went beyond that required by even the most demanding of lighthouse inspectors. The man worked relentlessly at keeping the station in pristine order.

Even so, it's believed Osborne relented somewhat in his search for a helper. He initially hoped to recruit a man with experience—perhaps a seasoned assistant from another lighthouse or a lightship, or else a master or first mate of a tender who at least had worked for the Lighthouse Establishment. But John Stevens had no knowledge of the intricate workings of light stations, no familiarity with the sea, no lifesaving skills or hard-earned keeper's wisdom. In fact, he had no experience at all, save for filling in on occasion for the keepers on Morris Island.

But he seemed to have a sincere interest in learning. Or at least that's what keeper Osborne told himself, to keep from admitting he'd hired the man out of sheer desperation. It was not in Osborne's nature to put his own needs before the station's. It was not a matter of physical and mental exhaustion, he insisted. It was more a matter of maintaining vigilance. Surely, Stevens could keep his eyes trained on the water for emergencies and occasionally scrub a few windows. Why, old man Gould, who tended the first lighthouse on the island, had entrusted a slave to assist him. If Lampblack, the Negro boy, had done it, then so could John Stevens.

Legend has it that, sometime thereafter, Stevens fell in love with Osborne's wife, causing an impasse between the men that would later end in murder. Though little is known about the love affair, some say it resulted from a closeness in age that the keeper himself did not share with his young wife.

Wearing gray-striped trousers and an unbleached muslin shirt, Stevens appeared to the keeper to be lacking any semblance of military decorum. Though it's unknown exactly when lighthouse keepers officially began wearing uniforms, Osborne took strict care in dressing for the part, and he expected the same of his assistant. Osborne, like sailors of the time, even stitched his own uniform by hand. During their interview, he had asked Stevens how proficient he was with needle and thread.

"Not very handy, I'm afraid, sir," Stevens had responded.

"Humph," Osborne said, having guessed as much. Standing to his full height, he studied Stevens, thinking hard before he spoke. He scanned the width of the younger man's shoulders, took a look at the size of his hands, noted the evenness of his teeth. Though there was plenty about John Stevens that gave the keeper pause, he hired him anyway. Extending a hand that was more warning than welcome, he said, "See my wife about being properly fitted for a uniform."

"Will do, sir," Stevens replied.

"Mind you, it'll be coming from your pay."

"Aye, sir. Very good."

And with that, the two struck an agreement.

"I'll man the light at night till you've acquired an eye I can trust," Osborne said. "But I expect that won't be long, will it, Stevens?"

"No, sir. Indeed, it won't."

Legend holds that Stevens tried desperately to please Osborne. But regardless of how often he polished the windows in the lantern room, the assistant could not satisfy his overseer. "Tell me, Stevens. Are these windows clean?"

"Yes, sir. They're spotless."

"Spotless?"

Growing weary of Osborne's contempt, Stevens eventually began to reply in kind: "Are they not spotless, sir? Have I not rid the glass of every particle of lint, every stray bit of dust, for pity's sake? Show me. Show me if there is even a speck I've overlooked!"

And of course, Osborne did. "There," he would say, pointing to a far corner or a spot overhead. "I saw it immediately. How it didn't jump out at you as well is a mystery. Perhaps you're tired. Or were you simply too busy carrying on conversations with my wife all night through the speaking tube?"

"How dare you accuse me of such a thing!"

"Do you deny it, Stevens?"

And the truth was, the young assistant couldn't. The speaking tube was Stevens's lifeline to the woman he loved but could not have.

"I will not stand for it," Osborne warned. "Do you think I cannot see what is right before me? I have a trained eye for seeing what others fail to see, Stevens. And I will not tolerate your smudged fingerprints on my windows or anywhere else. Do I make my intentions clear enough?"

"You see nothing," Stevens spat back. "You're a blind man."

What started with a fitting for a uniform grew into the kindling of unspoken desires as Stevens and the keeper's wife passed each other coming and going inside the house, where a staircase led from the main residence downstairs to the assistant's room above.

Little is known of the details of their relationship. Still less is remembered about the keeper's wife's life, although legend holds she was filled with a vitality that Osborne himself lacked. She was drawn to the processions of free blacks dancing their way to the river for baptisms, and might even have joined them if not for her husband's fear of yellow fever. She learned to speak the Gullah dialect. And when her husband complained of aches and pains, she told him to stuff a sprig of Spanish moss in the heel of his shoe. "Nonsense," Osborne said.

John Stevens and the keeper's wife worked side by side in the garden. Sometimes, sitting on the front porch, they shucked baskets of corn or snapped beans.

"Come inside, my dear," Osborne begged his wife. "I fear it isn't safe to sit outdoors at dusk. The mosquitoes, you know."

"But it's perfectly divine," his wife replied.

Osborne then used his authority to separate the pair. Turning to Stevens, he said, "Come with me. I need your assistance in the watch room."

No one knows how long things carried on in this manner, but the story goes that after Stevens had been at the station approximately two years, tensions between the men finally flared out of control. Some say that Osborne pushed Stevens too far in insisting the windows were not clean enough. But others swear heated words were exchanged concerning the clandestine affair between Stevens and the keeper's wife. At any rate, the altercation began in the lighthouse tower. After a fierce volley of obscenities, Osborne is said to have run down out of the tower, angry as the devil. Stevens, too, is said to have been passionately riled. So down the tower steps he went as well, following closely on Osborne's tail.

When Stevens stepped outside, he found Osborne waiting for him with pistol in hand, ready to kill him dead. With a rush of adrenaline, Stevens ran into the keepers' quarters and soon came back brandishing a weapon himself, a double-barreled shotgun loaded with buckshot. The facts of what happened next are sketchy, but the story holds that Osborne made a sudden move toward Stevens and the assistant pulled the trigger, wounding the keeper in the abdomen.

"Oh, dear Lord," Stevens said in disbelief. "What have I done?" Rushing to Osborne's aid, he tried to stop the bleeding. The keeper's wife ran outside at the sound of the gun and found her husband mortally wounded. "It was an accident," Stevens told her. "He needs a doctor."

The young assistant supposedly transported his overseer to the hospital in Brunswick. Afterward, he returned to the lighthouse and carried out his duties. A few days later, however, the keeper died, and Stevens was arrested.

Strangely, a malevolent storm kicked up just at that time. The authorities in Brunswick agreed that John Stevens should be allowed to return to St. Simons Island to man the light during the storm, half expecting that when it was over, the assistant would have gone missing, never to be found.

But to their amazement, they found him vigorously scrubbing the windows inside the lantern room and behaving strangely. "What's the matter, Stevens?" they asked. "You look like you've seen a ghost."

Apparently, he had.

The assistant claimed at his trial that he'd only defended himself. Though he was acquitted of all charges, he was sentenced to a punishment worse than being imprisoned— he was nearly driven mad by the ghost of Fred Osborne. Staying on at the light station until a replacement could be found, Stevens began hearing strange sounds—dull footfalls slowly slogging across the station yard, then mounting the cast-iron stairs of the tower. Inside, the footsteps echoed. But whenever Stevens peered down the spiral stairs, he saw nothing. Then, returning to the lantern room, he found streaks in the glass he was sure he could not have overlooked. Consequently, he became obsessed with polishing the windows.

But the story doesn't end there. Carl Svendsen, a later keeper at St. Simons, claimed that he and his wife also heard the spectral footsteps of someone climbing the tower. Many times during their twenty-some years at the lighthouse, they heard Fred Osborne's ghost. Their dog, Jinx, reacted oddly, howling and staring at one spot whenever the ghost was nearby. Whenever Mrs. Svendsen felt cold drafts pass through the kitchen in the keepers' quarters, Jinx, sound asleep, would suddenly stir and bristle as he watched something unseen pass in front of him. If the spirit came too near, Jinx became defensive, barking and growling as if his life depended on it.

No one knows what became of John Stevens or the keeper's wife. But islanders say the finicky ghost of Fred Osborne still watches over the lighthouse at St. Simons Island, having reclaimed his duties for eternity.

In colonial times, St. Simons Island was known as Fort Simons, after a military garrison was established there to fortify St. Simons Sound and the southern tip of the island. During the Battle of Bloody Marsh in 1742, however, Spaniards destroyed the fort and left the island in ruins.

Following that, a plantation owner named John Couper bought the property and renamed it Couper Point. In 1804, he sold four acres of land to the government for one dollar in order to build a light station at the south end of the island. Three years later, the Treasury Department hired James Gould to build a lighthouse. Gould's design called for a brick tower, but the Treasury Department scaled the project back, forcing Gould to work with a material commonly used to build slave cabins on the island—tabby, a mixture of crushed oyster shells, lime, sand, and water. In 1810, the seventy-five-foot tower was activated, and Gould was appointed as the first light keeper, a position he held for twenty-seven years. In 1857, the light was refitted with a third-order Fresnel lens.

During the Civil War, Confederate soldiers established Fort Brown on the island. They later evacuated it and blew up the lighthouse to prevent the advancing Union army from benefiting from the beacon. In 1867, plans were made to build a new light station. Charles Cluskey, a prominent Savannah architect, was hired to design the lighthouse and oversee the construction. Cluskey had helped renovate the United States Capitol building. Unfortunately, he never saw the lighthouse completed. He died of malaria in 1871, a year before the second tower was finished. Many of his builders suffered the same fate.

In 1972, the light station was deeded to Glynn County and listed on the National Register of Historic Places. For three years, volunteers of the Coastal Georgia Historical Society worked to restore the buildings. In 1984, the 104-foot tower was opened to climbers. It stands behind a beautiful

Victorian-style keepers' house built of Savannah "gray" brick. The walls are twelve inches thick, and the floors are heart pine. Inside, visitors will find the Museum of Coastal History downstairs and a mock-up of the keepers' quarters upstairs.

To reach the St. Simons Island Lighthouse, turn off US 17 in Brunswick onto the F. J. Torras Causeway, a toll road. After crossing the bridge onto St. Simons, turn right on King's Way and continue past the airport, on the left. At the next traffic signal, turn right on Mallory Street. Go a block to Beachview Drive, then turn left. At Twelfth Street, turn right into the lighthouse parking lot. For more information, call 912-638-4666.

St. Augustine Light
© 2004 Bob and Sandra Shanklin, the "Lighthouse People"

The Little Sisters
of St. Augustine

St. Augustine Light
Anastasia Island, Florida

"Whose loves
Are dearer than the natural bond of sisters."

William Shakespeare, *As You Like It*

St. Augustine is touted as being the oldest city in America, predating Jamestown, Virginia, by forty-two years and the landing at Plymouth Rock by fifty-five. The fabled city of Ponce de Leon's elusive Fountain of Youth, St. Augustine, almost twice as old as the United States itself, has a storied past steeped in legends and Old World mystique.

Of the numerous places said to be haunted there, one of the most beautiful and popular is the St. Augustine Lighthouse. Built in 1874, the station takes its charm from the romantic Spanish city that hosts it. Surrounded by a grove of live oak trees, the black-and-white-striped tower rises 165 feet and is capped by a striking red lantern room overlooking the sea.

The current tower is the second built on Anastasia Island. Its predecessor was a wooden watchtower constructed in the 1580s to guard against pirates. In 1673, the Castillo de San Marcos, a fortress built of limestone, crushed oyster shells, and coral, assumed the role of defending the city. At that time, a new lighthouse was constructed using the same materials. In 1824, after Spain ceded Florida to the United States, Elias Wallen was hired to convert the old tower into Florida's first official lighthouse. It stood only thirty feet above sea level, however, and needed to be made taller. The tower was raised to fifty-two feet sometime between 1824 and 1855, when a fourth-order Fresnel lens replaced the inefficient Winslow Lewis lamps and reflectors.

Even after such improvements, though, mariners complained the light wasn't sufficient. To make matters worse, beach erosion threatened the old sentinel. In 1871, plans were finally put in motion to replace Wallen's lighthouse with the tower that stands in St. Augustine today. Paul Petz, designer of the Library of Congress, was commissioned to oversee the project. His specs called for a 165-foot brick tower with a first-order Fresnel lens. The project cost $110,000. The new lamp was lit on October 15, 1874.

But all did not go well during the construction. Tragedy struck on July 10, 1873.

On that beautiful summer day, Mary and Eliza Pittee were playing with another little girl from the island. Eliza grew interested in a railway wagon used to haul supplies from the dock to the lighthouse construction site, where her father worked as the foreman. Mary, a little older, didn't like the idea. Their father would be cross if they made trouble while he was working.

"I am the captain of this vessel," Eliza proclaimed. Before

Mary could object, Eliza and the other girl climbed inside the wagon. "What's our course, lieutenant?"

"I'm the lieutenant," Mary said, stepping forward, grabbing up the hem of her skirt, and climbing aboard.

Pitched at a slight decline, the tracks ran in a straight line through a dense forest to the beach, where lighthouse building supplies were unloaded from boats.

"You take the crow's nest, ensign," Eliza told the other girl.

"Aye, captain."

"We'll make for the isle of Cuba," said Mary. "Here's our line of position."

"Cuba!" said Eliza. "Weigh anchor!"

And in the spirit of adventure—before she realized what she was doing—Mary released the hand brake that held the wagon in place.

The wagon inched forward, lazing along at first. Soon, it whooshed over the rails like a steam engine, however, much to the intrepid Eliza's delight. "Whee!" she yelled as the wagon rumbled over the tracks and under the canopy of trees.

But Mary was uneasy. Being the elder daughter, she knew her father would hold her accountable should an accident happen. She looked for a way to make the thing stop. "Eliza!" she shouted. "Help me with the brake."

The younger girl ignored her. She wasn't interested in ending their fun just yet. Eliza and her other companion leaned forward, craning their necks for a view of the ocean—which came into sight rather quickly, they began to notice, as their weight propelled the wagon toward the dock. Alone, Mary tugged with all her might on the hand brake, to no avail.

Only then did Eliza and the other girl realize the danger they were in. All three began screaming for help—and lamenting the punishment they were surely in for, once the sisters' father reached them. "Hold on!" Mary yelled, assuming command of the runaway car, bracing herself for dear life, fearing the wagon would not hold to the tracks but crash and plunge them to their early deaths in the sea.

It was a dead reckoning, in a manner of speaking.

The idea of jumping out of the wagon came to the girls too late. The ride was furious and short. Still, they tried, clambering one on top of the other to throw a leg over the side and leap. But when the wagon reached the dock, it jerked to a whiplash halt and pitched all three girls into the water. None could swim. The community was devastated when the girls were found several hours later.

Visitors and volunteers at the lighthouse have seen the little sisters Mary and Eliza since, however—playing tag and chasing each other up the tower stairs, or else giggling and running on the catwalk surrounding the lantern room on top. Now and again, people see a face staring somberly from a window in the keeper's house, a dark-haired girl wearing a crimson-colored dress and a sad expression.

After a mysterious fire gutted the keeper's residence in 1970, the property fell into disrepair until the Junior Service League took on the project of restoring it in 1980. Workers staying overnight in the house reported that they "sensed things." Some awoke during the night and found a little girl dressed in Victorian clothes standing over them. Once seen, she simply vanished.

Other people talk about little Eliza, the prankster. Some say if you're ever in an upstairs room in the keeper's house, you shouldn't be surprised if she touches your arm or locks the door. You might even hear her laughing at you.

Still others believe both sisters are responsible for locking the doors. Occasionally, visitors step inside a room, only to hear the door across the way suddenly shut and lock.

To reach the St. Augustine Lighthouse from I-95, take Exit 318, head east for approximately five miles, and turn right on US 1. Turn left at King Street, cross the Bridge of Lions, and you'll see the lighthouse on your left. Proceed south on Anastasia Boulevard/FL A1A to Red Cox Road and turn left. The St. Augustine Lighthouse and Museum is on the left.

For more information, call 904-829-0745 or visit www.staugustinelighthouse.com.

Pensacola Light
© *2004 Courtesy of Pensacola Bay CVB*

THE POLTERGEIST

OF PENSACOLA

PENSACOLA LIGHT
PENSACOLA BAY, FLORIDA

"There are glances of hatred that stab and raise no
cry of murder; robberies that leave man or woman
forever beggared of peace and joy, yet kept secret
by the sufferer—committed to no sound except that
of low moans in the night."

George Eliot, *The Radical*

The deep waters of Pensacola Bay made western Florida
one of the most sought-after regions in the New World.
Discovered by Spanish explorers in 1516, Florida was later
controlled by the British and the French before it was finally taken by Andrew Jackson in 1818 and made a terri-
tory of the United States.

Considered one of best ports in the Gulf of Mexico,

Pensacola Bay was illuminated by the lightship *Aurora Borealis* beginning in late June 1823, until a permanent light station could be built on a ridge across from the western tip of nearby Santa Rosa Island. The meager light the ship supplied proved ineffective and unreliable, as the vessel could not stay moored in the choppy waters outside the bay. Therefore, the first lighthouse at Pensacola went up in a flash. Congress authorized the construction in March 1823. By December 22, 1824, the first light keeper was making his rounds. The project cost a mere $5,725. It took barely two months to build the tower and an additional two days to throw together a keeper's house. Though there are no known drawings or pictures of the first light station at Pensacola, records in the National Archives suggest it was most likely built of stone or brick. Archaeologists hired to dig the site in 1997 found evidence suggesting the tower was indeed constructed of brick. But although the contract between the government and the builder stipulated that the keeper's residence also be built of stone or brick, evidence from the dig indicates it was most likely a wood-frame structure resting on brick piers.

Not that it mattered to the young New Englander hired to man the station. Jeremiah Ingraham found his new quarters and the isolation of tending the lighthouse perfectly suited to his bachelor lifestyle. He could tell he was going to like the tropical climate of Florida and the serene backdrop of white beaches and cerulean waters. His salary was inadequate, a meager $137.50 per quarter. But since he was a man on his own, he would manage just fine.

And for two years, he did. The sea offered a bounty of mullet, drum, redfish, trout, pompano, sheepshead, oysters, clams—even turtles. And the growing season in Pensacola was long, allowing him to raise his own grapes, strawberries, raspberries, rice, pepper weed, green panic, pigweed. He even grew medicinal plants like spurge, hawthorn, and nightshade.

But by and by, he felt it was all too much for one man alone. He remembered how his mother had put up stores of canned goods and smoked meats when he was a boy in Massachusetts. His role had been to help his father fish and hunt wild game, and to that end, he was still an able angler and marksman. Turkeys and mallards ran rampant in the thickets around the light station. But the issue of how to store such bounty became a growing concern.

At Sunday worship, the pioneer families of Pensacola advised him to take a wife. And so he did. On August 31, 1826, Jeremiah Ingraham and Michaela Florentine Penalber were married before friends and family. By all accounts, they initially lived a good life. Within two years, the couple had its first child, a daughter, Irene. Albert came next, and then the baby, another boy. Michaela took naturally to motherhood and running a household. She expanded the small kitchen garden Jeremiah had tended alone. Now, they farmed three acres. And together, they fenced the rest of the land for livestock. On occasion, they bartered, trading a heifer when they had to for supplies they couldn't raise themselves. If white-tailed deer were running, Michaela urged Jeremiah to hunt. When he was successful, she butchered the animals herself and cured the meat.

But they had to feed the strapping young Negro boy living with them who helped tend the light, as well as Michaela's ailing father and their own growing family. There seemed never enough beef and venison. It wasn't long before the Ingraham budget became a source of heated contention.

"I don't know how you expect us to live this way," Michaela complained, pressuring Jeremiah to seek odd jobs. His duties at the lighthouse left him plenty of time, she argued. And besides, she felt that she could look after the light as well as he could, a point she seemed proud to make.

Jeremiah felt his role as light keeper was being challenged.

"But I am the one assigned to this post," he replied. "It is my duty to oversee the station."

"Nobody cares who does it," she contended, "so long as someone does. You're entitled to feed your own family, aren't you?"

Jeremiah didn't see an urgent need to work unceasingly. After all, Albert had clay marbles and his own small saddle for riding horses. Irene had a china doll. They had writing slates for school. His wife had plenty of straight pins for sewing and a good brass wedding band.

But in time, Jeremiah couldn't deny that he was no longer making ends meet, though he worked like a brute. He rose early to fill the eighteen lamps with whale oil and to replace the fragile glass chimneys that broke too often. Every two hours, he climbed the eighty-foot tower near the edge of the bluff to pull the weights that wound the clockwork mechanism that rotated the light. When necessary, he painted the Georgian-style arched lintels over the doors and windows of the lighthouse, replaced busted slates, repaired the glazed double-paned windows. There were hinges and thumb latches to oil, water to draw from the brick-lined well. And the hunting, fishing, and farming seemed never to end.

And that was just the regular routine. The first lighthouse was thought by mariners to be too similar to the neighboring light at Mobile, Alabama. And because of the trees on nearby Santa Rosa Island, it wasn't visible far enough at sea. In addition to that, the tower's substandard masonry drew dampness that weakened the structure and demanded continual maintenance. To top it all off, the spiral staircase was hazardous because it had no railing.

Still, the tower stood for over thirty years, during which time it was tenured mostly by the Ingrahams.

No one is sure why the couple's bickering steadily grew over the course of their marriage. Some say Jeremiah could not satisfy his wife no matter how hard he worked, so he resigned himself to doing nothing beyond what suited him at the moment. He kept up his lighthouse duties. He fished with his daughter and rode horses with his son. But more and more often, he let chores fall to Michaela and the freed slave she'd hired to help them.

To outsiders, however, the couple maintained the appearance of happiness for years. But Michaela, for one, could not have been more discontented. Legend holds that, one night while her husband lay sleeping, she crept down to the kitchen for a knife used to butcher livestock. By then, the children were grown and married, and the house was perfectly empty save for the two of them. Jeremiah was in the habit of waking every two hours through the night to wind the clockwork mechanism of the lighthouse. He'd conditioned his body to fall asleep quickly between shifts and to rest soundly. Nothing could wake him—not footfalls on the stairs or the rattle of cupboard drawers in the kitchen as Michaela searched for the sharpest blade in the house. She then walked boldly back to the bedroom and stabbed her husband in the back. Blood soaked the linens of their conjugal bed. As Jeremiah fought for his life, he jerked backward and fell to the wooden floor with a dead thud.

Some people say Michaela stood over her husband and watched him breathe his dying breath. When it was over, she hid the evidence of his brutal murder and reported his death as a hunting accident. She then assumed her husband's position as lighthouse keeper at Pensacola and served the post until her own death years later.

But according to long-told stories, Michaela's tenure at the light station was even more plagued with problems than her husband's had been. Most notably, the clockwork mechanism stopped working in the late 1840s. To keep the strobe flashing, Michaela and her Negro helper had to rotate the lens by hand. Eventually, she had to hire two men to do that strenuous work until repairs could be made. What's more, the ghost of Jeremiah Ingraham might have unnerved her. Some have speculated that Michaela was tormented by her husband's vengeful spirit—that she, like visitors today, witnessed objects being hurled through the air, heard ominous laughter in empty rooms of the house, saw silhouettes slither in front of the windows of the locked tower at night, smelled the distinct odor of pipe tobacco, and felt blasts of cold air in the house no matter how much she stoked the fire.

Though the old station has been replaced, people claim the bloodstain of Jeremiah Ingraham's murder shows through the floorboards of the upstairs bedroom of the current keeper's house, and that no amount of scrubbing will remove it—at least not for long. According to Emmitt Hatten, whose father manned the present station long after the Ingrahams were gone, his mother scrubbed the floor constantly, but the eerie stain always reappeared whenever the weather was damp. Though the floor is covered by a carpet, the stain is locked into the house for eternity. It often reappears in the unmistakable shape of a body, a reminder of the station's ghoulish past.

There's another thing Emmitt Hatten remembers about living at the lighthouse as a boy. "When I would go to pull the chains to keep the lens turning, I could hear human breathing," he told Coast Guard staffers. "I was certain that it wasn't mine, and I would stop and listen."

Emmitt isn't the only one to have experienced such hair-raising phenomena in the tower. More recently, a father and his two children visited the lighthouse. While they were touring the tower, the eight-year-old son stopped suddenly on the staircase. "What's the matter?" his father asked. The boy replied that someone had just whispered his name—Alex—in his ear.

When the Hattens lived at the lighthouse, they saw doors open and close by themselves. Frequently in the evening hours, Emmitt's family heard footsteps walking toward the front door of the keeper's house. Then the door would open and close, and the footsteps would continue toward the gate. Finally, the gate would open and close, and the footsteps would be heard no more.

And the doors will not stay locked. Coast Guard staff members have reported locking all the station doors at night and double-checking them before leaving, then returning the next morning to find them all unlocked.

Many people have smelled pipe tobacco in the tower, but one Coast Guardsman actually saw smoke. When he and two additional Guardsmen climbed the tower after hours on a different occasion, all three felt some other presence inside the tower. They searched but couldn't find another living soul.

Others have been startled by the sudden slamming of the hatch to the lantern room. Even visitors touring the lighthouse have heard it.

But perhaps the most chilling evidence of Jeremiah Ingraham's lingering presence comes from a volunteer and his wife who in the late 1980s were told to check the lighthouse because the light wasn't on. When they arrived, they heard footsteps pacing and a man cursing. After looking all over the premises and failing to find the source, the husband went to repair the light. But while he was gone, his wife continued hearing the disembodied voice cursing and pacing up and down the hallway inside the keeper's residence. At the exact moment she saw the light come on, the cursing and pacing abruptly stopped.

In 1852, the Lighthouse Board recommended that a taller structure be built at Pensacola. Congress authorized the plans in 1854 and allocated a budget five times greater than that of the original station. The new tower—160 feet tall upon its completion in 1858—was located a half-mile west of the old site. The Pensacola Light is the fourth-tallest brick tower in the country. The first keeper was Jeremiah and Michaela Ingraham's son-in-law, Joseph Palmes, who started on New Year's Day 1859.

During the Civil War, the Confederates dismantled the first-order Fresnel lens and drew fire to the tower from Union forces stationed across the bay at Fort Pickens. Cannon shot struck the lighthouse in several places, though no damage was found beyond the tower's outer wall. In 1863, the lighthouse was refitted with a fourth-order Fresnel lens. In 1869, a larger lens was installed. When the original first-order lens was later found, it was given to another lighthouse.

The tower has been struck by lightning at least twice and even survived a rare earthquake that hit Pensacola in 1886. The army added electricity to the station in 1939. Shortly thereafter, authority was transferred to the Coast Guard. The station was automated in 1965. In 1971, Gulf Islands National Seashore was created to preserve the unmanned light station, as well as neighboring Fort Pickens and Fort Barrancas.

To reach Pensacola Naval Air Station, where the current lighthouse and the site of the old light are located, take US 90 to FL 295S/New Warrington Road/Navy Boulevard. When you reach FL 292/Barrancas Avenue, turn right. About five miles after the main gate of the air station, turn left on FL 173 and follow it onto the base. Look for the lighthouse on your right after you pass the guard station. The air station is open to the public, although the lighthouse tower may be closed for holidays or restoration. For information about tours, contact the Florida Coast Guard Lighthouse Auxiliary Flotilla 17 by visiting www.uscgaux.org.

ACKNOWLEDGMENTS

I am most grateful for the support and encouragement of my husband, Bruce, whose devoted alliance is a constant source of amazement and the greatest gift in my life. I would also like to thank my parents, Willard and Nola Stanley, for telling me I could someday be the president and for believing in me when I said I'd found a somewhat different calling. Simply put, I owe them everything. I am especially indebted to my mom for traveling with me to lighthouses and for showing me how to walk up to strangers and talk to them. I'm also deeply appreciative of the creative advice of my sister Tammy Stanley Brown, who always answers the phone in the middle of the night, and for the love and encouragement of my brother John Stanley, who inspired my first-ever story and inspires me still. I'm also thankful for Danny Brown, beloved brother-in-law, who read my manuscript enthusiastically and offered his valuable opinion. Thank you.

I owe a special debt of gratitude to my Winston-Salem writers' group—Penelope Niven, Joy Beshears Hagy, and Ginger Hendricks—for reading many of the stories in this collection (as well as others) and offering their invaluable assistance in making them better. My life is blessed by their friendship and constant support.

I am also grateful for the friendship and encouragement of Jennifer Niven, whose work I admire greatly and with whom I feel a deep kinship. Thank you.

Thanks as well go to Susan Woodring, Priscilla Cutler, Karen McBryde, and Gwynyth Mislin—fellow writers and friends—for their careful reading and advice on these stories and others.

I send thanks as well to my best friend, Melissa Frazier Shrewsbury, for her friendship these many years since fifth grade and for encouraging my writing by reminding me of its lucrative possibilities.

For instilling in me a love of good ghost stories, I'm grateful to my father and his siblings—William Bowlsbey, Henry Bowlsbey, James Bowlsbey, Jack Bowlsbey, Condy Stanley, Paul Stanley, Mandy Triplett, and Cordelia Fitzwater—as well as to their mother, my grandmother Martha Cary. And I'm grateful as well that my mother has helped keep old tales alive in our family.

For photographs used in this book, I extend my thanks to Bob and Sandra Shanklin, the Lighthouse People. I am grateful as well to the many historians, curators, tourism professionals, and lighthouse friends and aficionados who helped me compile information useful in writing these stories. I'm especially indebted to Sheri Poftak with the Friends of Wood Island Lighthouse; Susan Perow, former curator at Seguin Island Light; Scott Price and Erma Hill at the United States Coast Guard Historian's Office; Kelly Grimm of the Outer Banks History Center; Joe and Barbara Conaty, who were kind enough to direct me to researchers and archivists at the Library of Congress, the National Archives, and the Smithsonian; Pam and Henry Griffin, for further assistance in narrowing down researchers; Robert Ellis and Susan Abbott at the National Archives; J. Dennis Robinson at SeacoastNH.com; Jeremy D'Entremont; Ann Mills at Bald Head Light; Paul Kayemba at Visit Florida; Alan Jonusas at the St. Augustine, Ponte Verdra, and the Beaches Convention and Visitors Bureau; Stacy Garrett at the Pensacola Bay Area Convention and Visitors Bureau; and Patrick Saylor with the Brunswick and the Golden Isles of Georgia Convention and Visitors Bureau.

Finally, I am deeply grateful to the staff of John F. Blair for their hard work in helping to shape this book and make it available to readers everywhere. Specifically, I'm indebted to Steve Kirk, an editor of the highest caliber; Debra Long Hampton, who designed the book's cover and perfected its layout; Kim Byerly, Anne Waters, and Ed Southern, who did a masterful job of marketing and promoting the book; and Carolyn Sakowski, who has taught me more than she might realize.

About the Author

Sheryl Monks grew up in rural Appalachia, where ghost stories are as much a part of the oral tradition as they are along the Atlantic coast. She graduated summa cum laude from Salem College and subsequently earned an MFA from Queens University. She is a recipient of the Northwest North Carolina Regional Artist Project Grant and a winner of the national Reynolds Price Short Fiction Award. She lives in Hamptonville, North Carolina, with her husband, Bruce.